SUJOK SEED HEALING

WONDERS OF SEEDS

DOCTOR ASHOK SETHI

Contents

Foreword

It is of utmost importance to be healthy. One cannot enjoy life without good health. Not only good physical health, but good health at all levels : physical, mental and spiritual, is required by everyone on this earth to enjoy life. There are various Holistic Sciences, which take care of us at holistic level, e.g. Naturopathy, Yog, etc.

SuJok Seed Therapy is one such Holistic Science, developed by Professor Park Jae Woo of South Korea. Prof. Park Jae Woo spent his life for the benefit of mankind in developing various other scientific theories, such as, Six Ki theory, Homo-system theory, Homo-Hetero theory, Eight Origin theory, Triorigin theory, Diamond Energy System theory, M Particle theory, Onnuri Twist Therapy, Triorigin Smile Meditation, Triorigin Taichi, Smile Gymnastics and Smile Taiji.

Su Jok Seed Healing contains the extracts taken from my books on Sujok Therapy, Advance Sujok Therapy and Master Sujok Therapy, so far as these relate to Sujok Seed Healing. So it teaches you basic Sujok concepts and some of advance Sujok concepts also. It teaches us not only to keep physically fit but also metaphysically fit.

This book is my humble attempt to popularise this great science. I am sure, once one goes through this book, one will be able to remain healthy (and I say holistically healthy) with little time, money and effort.

I am a teacher and have been teaching various Holistic Sciences for the past more than 2 decades. Usually I provide study material to the students. Study material is prepared after going through various books available on the subject. But, this subject is new and whatever literature is available is authored by Prof. Park Jae Woo himself. Only very few other authors have ventured into this subject. Hence,

I had to borrow a lot from the books by Prof. Park.

I once again salute to Prof. Park who has developed this great Holistic Science.

Errors, inadvertent or typographical, have a bad habit of appearing in the text inspite of lot of editing. I hope the readers would be kind enough to ignore them.

Doctor Ashok Sethi
President
International Academy of Holistic Sciences
84, Tilak Khand, Giri Nagar, Kalkaji, New Delhi-110019
Ph : 9811047247, 01143926765, 9625723446

CHAPTER ONE

INTRODUCTION TO SEED THERAPY

Seeds give life to plants. This provides evidence that energy of huge power is present in them in a latent form. Constant exchange of this latent energy with the environment takes place through the mechanism of energy respiration, owing to which the seed, as a source of life, can improve health of other living organisms.

The method of seed therapy was firstly presented in 1988 by the founder of Sujok Therapy, Prof Park Jae Woo.

This method of health regulation, natural and quite simple in uses gives remarkable results in practice. Positive changes in illness take place on application of seeds to painful points of the body. Effectiveness of this treatment is caused by the biological waves, radiated during the vital activity of seeds, which stimulate the active points, fill them with the energy of life and at the same time absorb their pathogenic energy.

Application of Seed Therapy is based on Sujok Therapy, where it tells you where to apply seeds. Sujok Therapy tells us that miniature projections of the human body are located on the hands and feet. So seed therapy can be carried out by influencing not only the affected parts of the body but also these points on the hands and feet (called the correspondence points (areas). The method is very efficient. Its application often has a stronger and quicker effect. So first we will study Sujok Therapy as it explains the various correspondence points as per Standard Correspondence System, Insect Correspondence System. This will enable us to locate the points where the seeds are to be applied.

Seeds of various plants differ in their properties, each of them having its distinctive features. So, when selecting seeds, along with the colour and shape of the seed, the properties of plants which grow from them should also be taken into account. If one succeeds in selecting the most suitable seed for application, it will make the result more manifest.

Although the Seed Therapy, by virtue of its simplicity and ease of application, can be employed by any person, but at the same time professional knowledge about the properties of various plants helps realize all potentialities of this method.

Let us first understand what is Sujok Therapy.

SuJok Therapy was developed by a South Korean scientist, Prof. Park Jae Woo.

It is a Holistic Science for maintenance of Holistic Health. A Holistic Science is one which takes care of the problems completely, i.e. at all levels : physical, mental and spiritual.

Su means a Hand and Jok means a Foot in Korean language. Hence, it is a therapy which makes use of hands and feet for treatment of diseases/disorders.

It is so simple that it is very easy to learn, it is 100% safe, without any side effects and is very effective. It is called a Magic Wand, which can be used anywhere at any place.

Earlier therapies which use hands and feet for treatment of diseases are Acupressure, Reflexology, etc. In Acupressure, the treatment points are called Acu-points; in Reflexology, these are called Reflex points; in Su Jok Therapy, these are called Correspondence points.

What is a correspondence point : The first part of Sujok Therapy is an advanced version of acupressure.

According to Sujok principles our hands and feet are complete replica of our bodies. Any malfunctioning in any part of body results in a tender spot on the hand or foot, which is called its correspondence point. Once this point is stimulated, treated, it can cure the malfunctioning of the body part. Our body functions with a kind of energy, called Qi, Ki, Chi, Jeevani Shakti, Pran Vayu, etc. When this is blocked in the body, it makes that part where it is blocked, malfunction. When this blockage is removed, the person gets cured. And this is done with this Therapy.

This method can be used to diagnose a disease also. For example, if you feel pain at some point in hands or feet, find out which is the body part whose correspondence point is this. Then you can be sure that this body part is not functioning properly.

Once we understand the entire structure of our body, it can be mapped on hands and feet, enabling us to understand location of the correspondence points on our hands and feet very easily. This is what we are going to learn.

Seeds are applied or affixed on the particular correspondence points with a surgical tape.

How was Sujok Therapy discovered :

While doing research, Prof. Park found out the following similarities between the organs of our body and hands/feet.

Finding these similarities led Prof Park to think that the Almighty has given us hands and feet to take care of body ailments. That is how, various Correspondence Systems were developed.

1 Number of protruding Parts in our body : We all know that our body has five outstanding parts: the head, two arms and two legs. Similarly, our hand has five fingers that stand out of the palm. (Fig. 1)

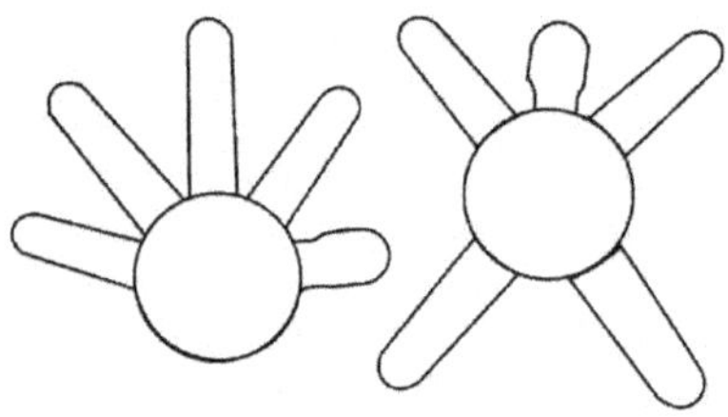

Fig. 1

2. Levels of the protruding parts of our body: In our body the head is topmost, and arms in the outermost position, with legs in the lowest position in between arms. Fig. 2

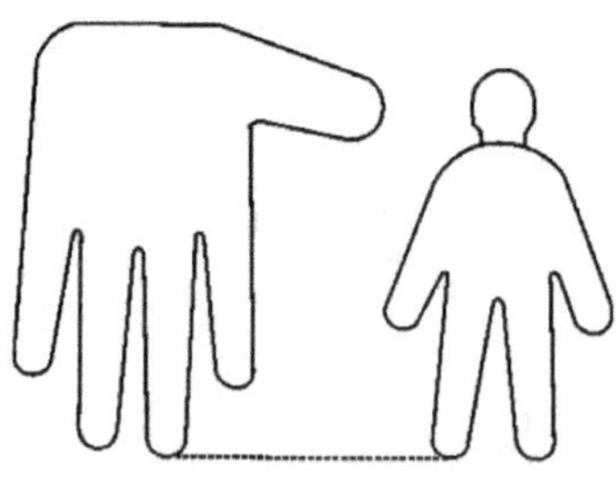

Fig 2

If we observe our hand, we can easily find the similarities here. The hand has the thumb in the topmost position, with the forefinger and little finger on the outside, and the third and fourth fingers are the lowest, in between them.

3. Directions of the protruding parts : The head is turned up looking skyward, while arms and legs are parallel and directed toward the ground. Similarly, in the hand, direction of the thumb is upwards, whereas the fingers are downwards. (Fig. 3)

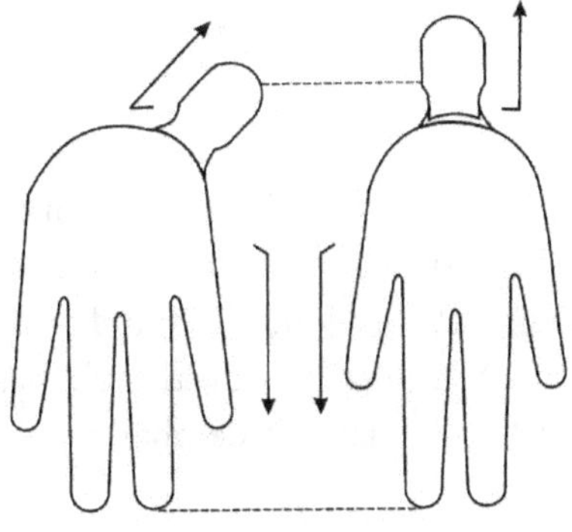

Fig. 3

4. Size of protruding parts : The head is the shortest and broadest protruding part of the body; similarly, the thumb in the hand is the shortest and broadest. In our body the legs are the longest parts; similarly, the third and fourth fingers are the longest. In our body, the arms are of middle size; similarly, the forefinger and little finger are of middle size. Fig 4

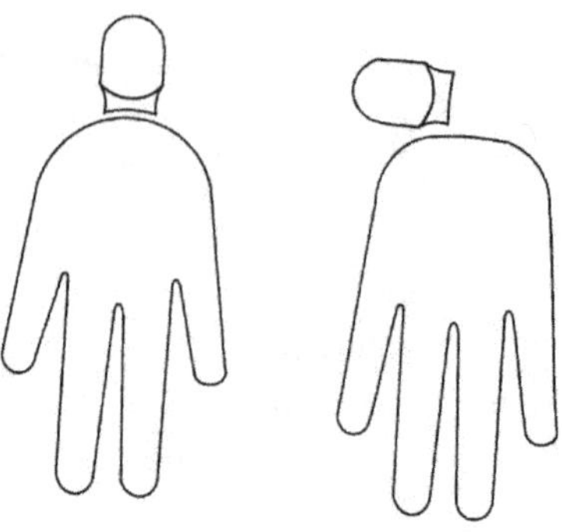

Fig. 4

5. Number of segments of protruding parts: In our body, the head is of two parts : the head proper and the neck. An arm and a leg have three parts each, separated by joints (shoulder, forearm and hand; thigh, ankle and foot). Similarly, our thumb has two phalanxes, while the other four fingers have three phalanxes each. (Fig. 5)

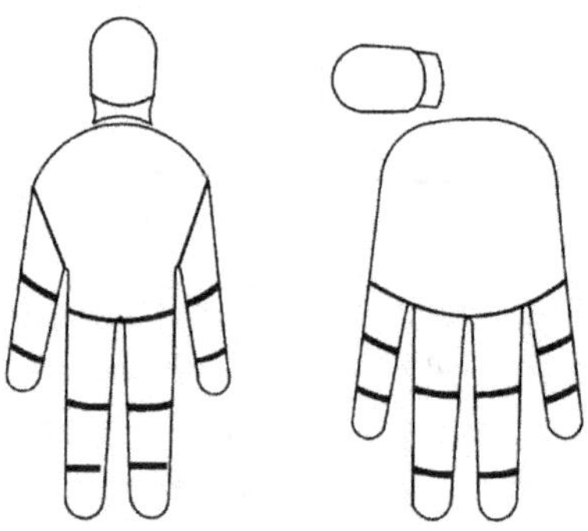

Fig. 5

6. Shape of Thumb : The head of our body and the thumb of our hand have similar shapes. (Fig. 6)

Fig. 6

7. Importance of the Thumb : In our body, the head is the controller of the entire body and extremities, through the Nervous System. Similarly, our thumb can easily reach the palms and all fingers. It is important for holding things. Hence, it can also control all the fingers. **(Fig. 7 and Fig. 8)**

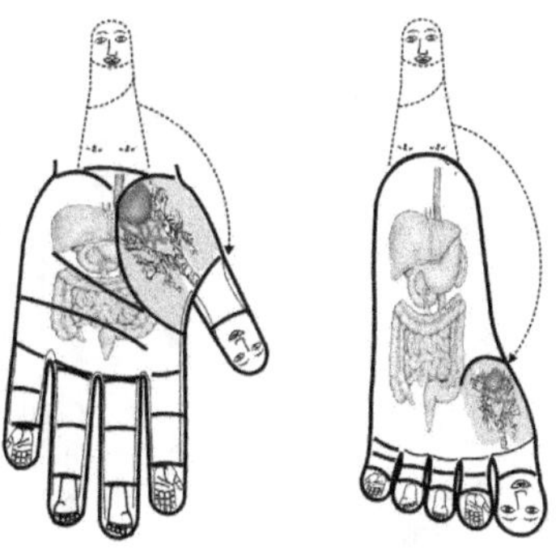

Left Hand Left Foot

The above similarities clearly reveal that our hands/feet are similar to our bodies, the only exception seems to be the thumb. But just imagine the thumb as in the figures below and our hands/feet become exactly similar to our bodies.

Correspondence Systems :

As already mentioned, Su means Hand and Jok means Foot. It would seem that the correspondence system will be limited to hands and feet. But it is not so. Sujok therapy is a very advanced therapy and it contains various correspondence systems. Seen from their respective angles, all remote points work very well.

First of all, we would study the Basic Correspondence System of hand and foot. Then the Insect Correspondence System.

Basic Correspondence System:

Before we go to the Basic Correspondence System, see the following figures which show you the similarities between body segments and hands and feet. (Fig 9)

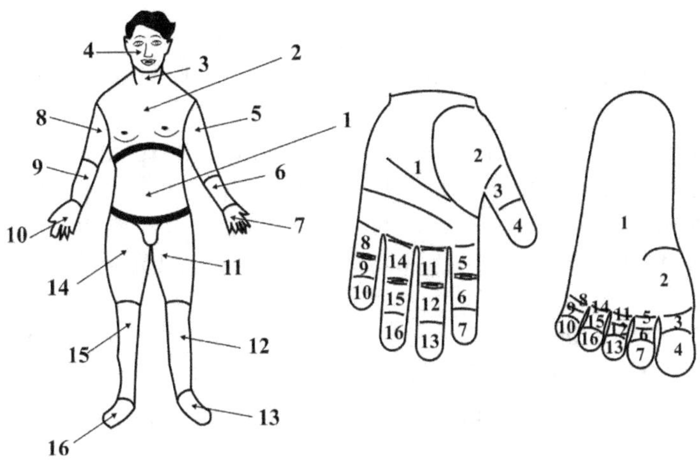

Fig. 9

Basic System of Correspondence of the Hand :

The Basic Correspondence System of hand and foot deals with the entire body being represented on the hands and feet, i.e. on the palms and fingers (front and back both) on the hand; and on the soles and toes (front and back) on the feet. **Fig. 10 and 11**

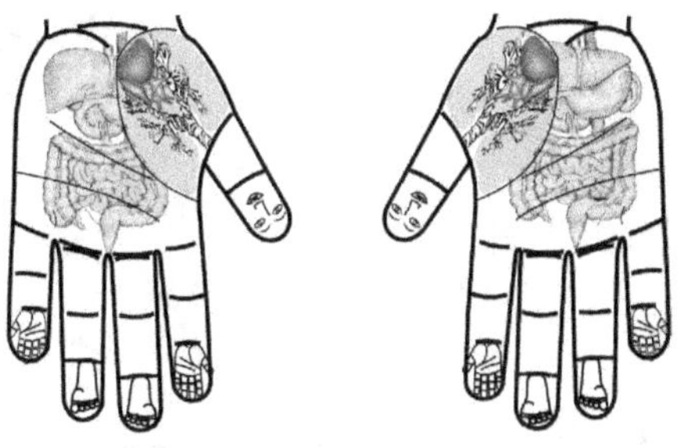

Left Hand Right Hand

The protrusion on the palm below the thumb corresponds to the chest, and the palm as a whole corresponds to the abdomen region.

Observe the following figures and you would understand, the Index Finger of the right hand and the Little Finger of the left hand corresponds to the right arm. The Index Finger of the left hand and the Little Finger of the right hand corresponds to the left arm.

The Middle Finger of the right hand and the Ring Finger of the left hand corresponds to the right leg. The Middle Finger of the left hand and the Ring Finger of the right hand corresponds to the left leg. (Fig. 12)

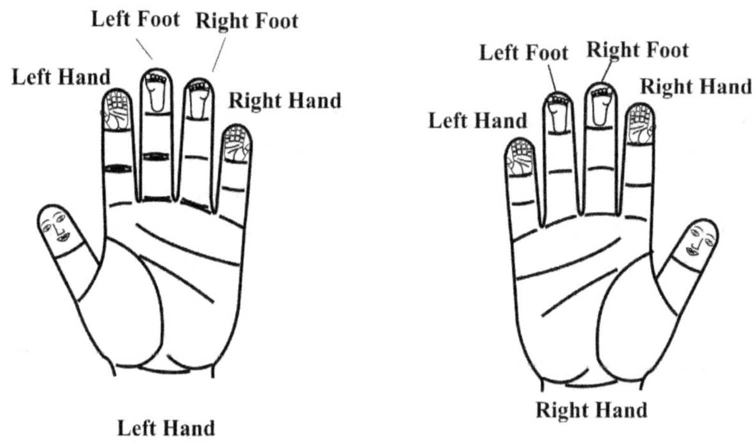

Fig. 12

Basic System of Correspondence of the Foot:

As is clear from, the correspondence system of the foot is based on the same principles as the basic system of correspondence of the hand. **(Fig 13)**

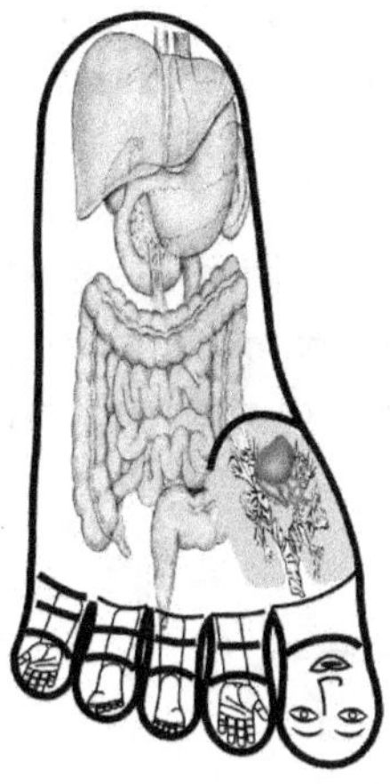 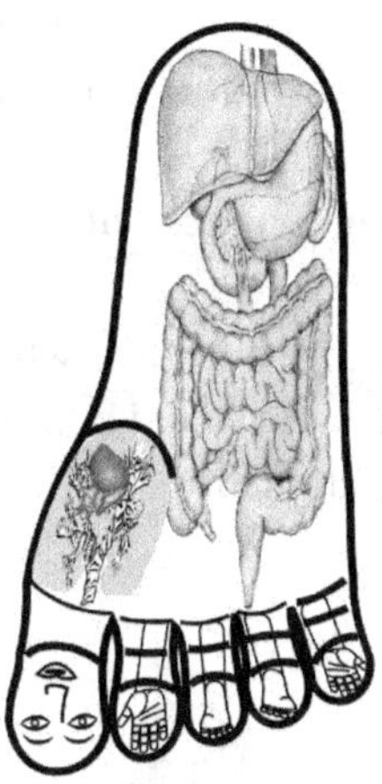

Left Foot Right Foot

Thus, contrary to earlier therapies, this system has complete body in each hand/foot, i.e. we have 4 bodies (two in hands and two in feet) to work for treatment, as per the Basic Correspondence System.

Yin and Yang Concept:

In order to locate the exact correspondence points as per this system, it is important to understand Yin and Yang concept.

Everything in this universe has Yin and Yang sides, like darkness and brightness; male and female; happiness and sorrow, etc. Yin means negative energy and Yang means positive energy. The merger of Yin and Yang is called Chi, the energy. Yin and Yang are supplement to each other; without the presence of two, the single one has just got no significance. In Yin there is little of Yang; and in Yang, there is little of Yin.

Imbalance of Yin and Yang causes diseases in our bodies. The hand is Yang, the foot is Yin. In stimulating both of them at the same time one can do treatment in the harmony of Yin and Yang.

Yin and Yang Surfaces of the body

The surface of the body which is not exposed to the sunlight is called the Yin surface, i.e. inner surfaces of the hands (palms) and feet (soles), etc. (Fig. 14A)

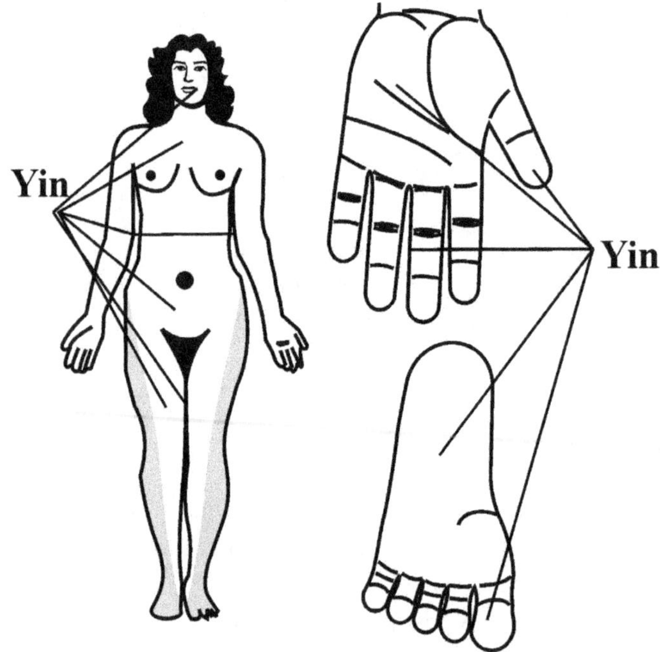

Fig. 14A

The surface of the body which is exposed to the sunlight is the Yang surface, i.e. outer surfaces of hands and feet, as well as the buttocks, back and backside of the head. (Fig. 14B)

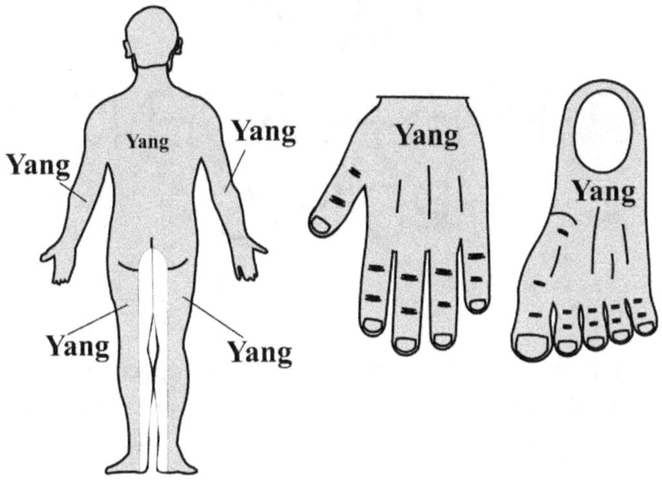

Fig 14B

CHAPTER TWO

BASIC CORRESPONDENCE POINTS

Following figures show the major correspondence points of the body organs/parts in the hand/foot, as per Basic/Standard/ Original Correspondence System :

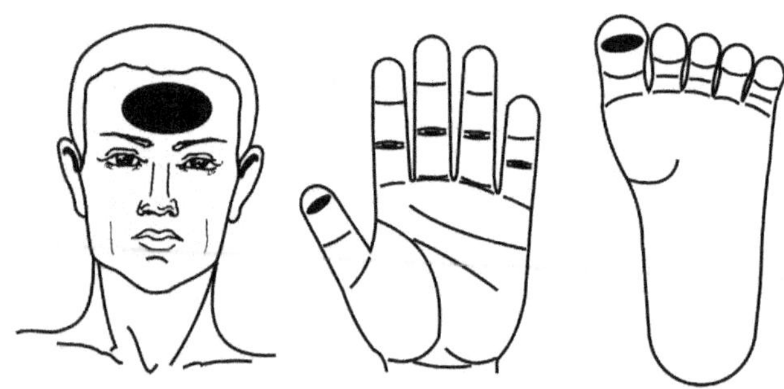

Forehead (Fig. 15)

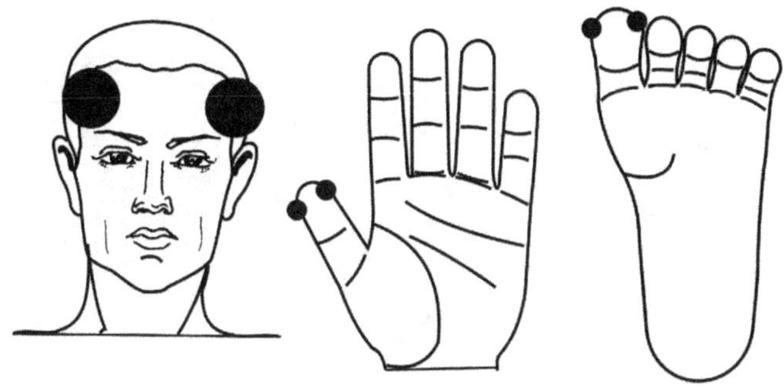

Temporal Areas (Fig. 16)

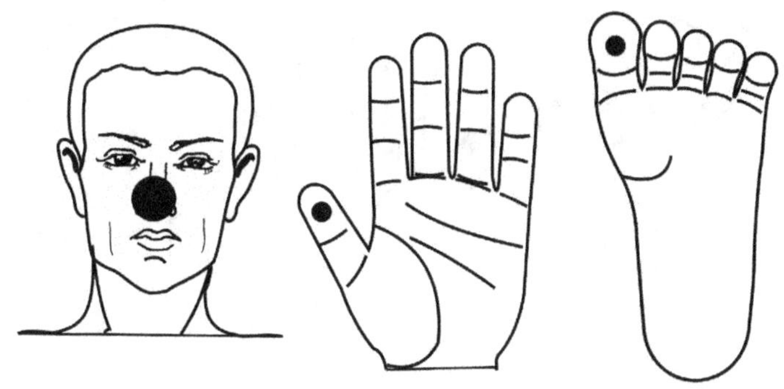

Nose (Fig . 17)

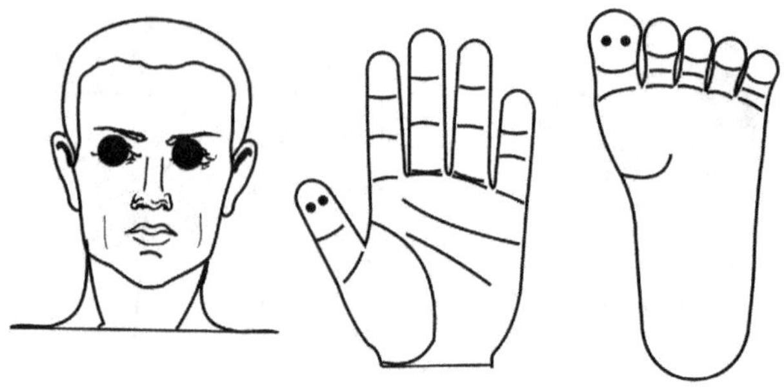

Eyes (Fig. 18)

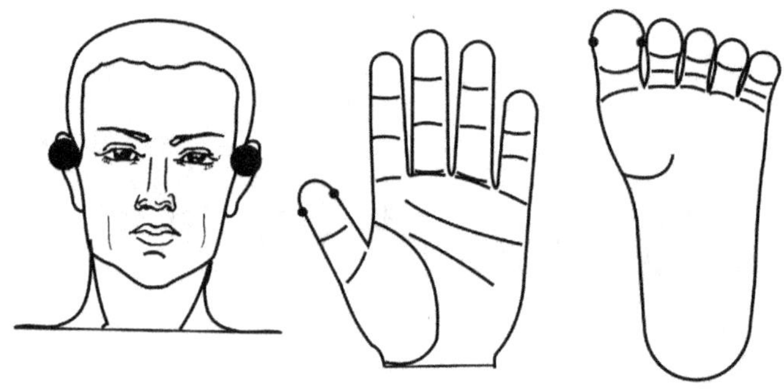

Ears (Fig. 19)

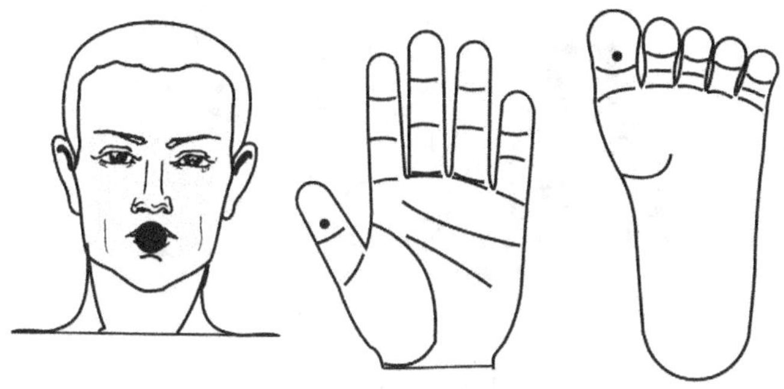

Mouth, Gums & Teeth (Fig. 20)

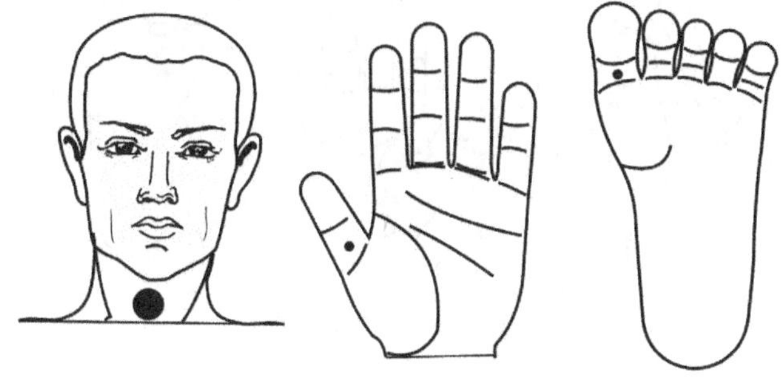

Larynx (Fig. 21)

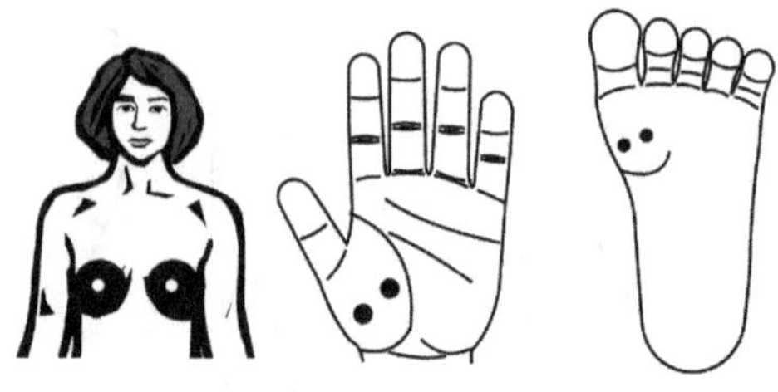

Breasts (Fig. 22)

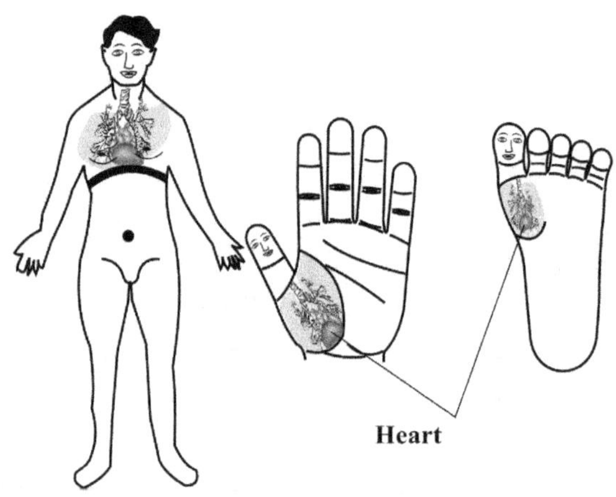

Heart (Fig. 23)

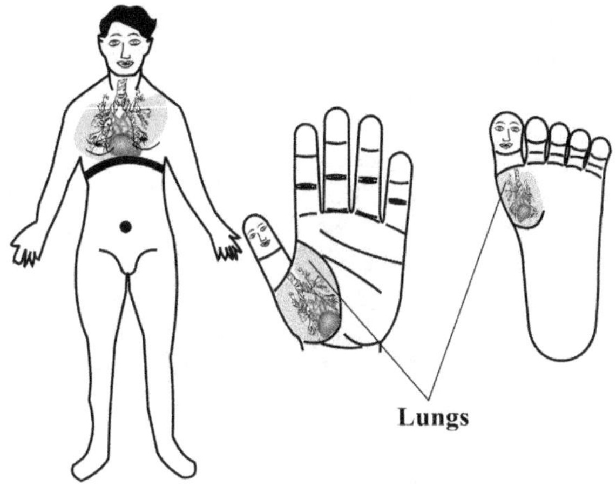

Lungs

Lungs (Fig. 24)

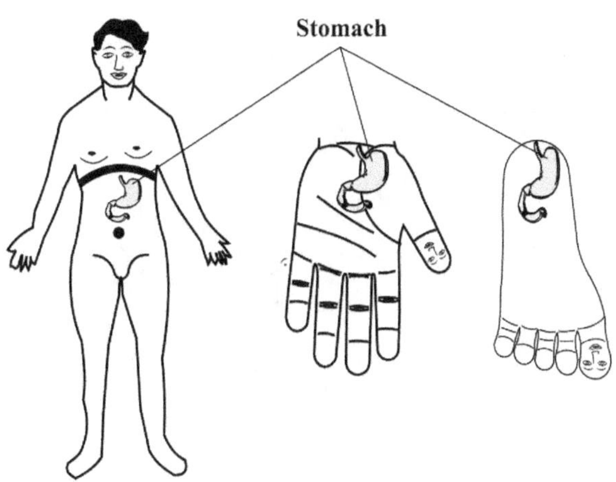

Stomach

Stomach : Fig. 25

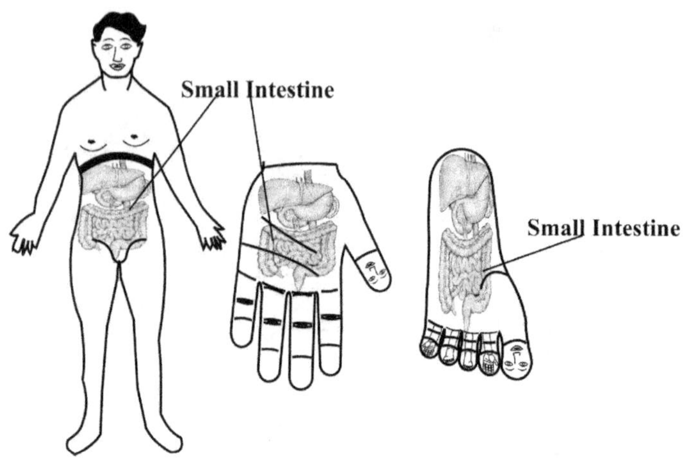

Small Intestine (Fig. 26)

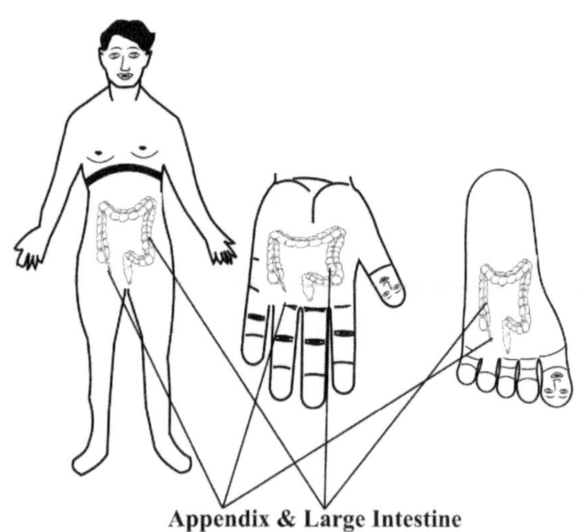

Appendix and Large Intestine (Fig. 27)

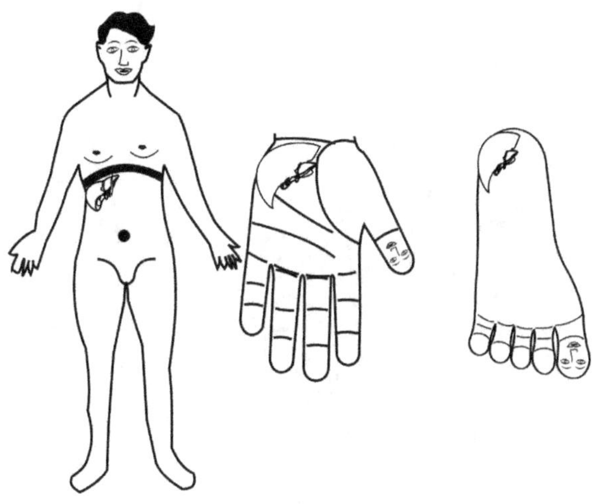

Fig. 28

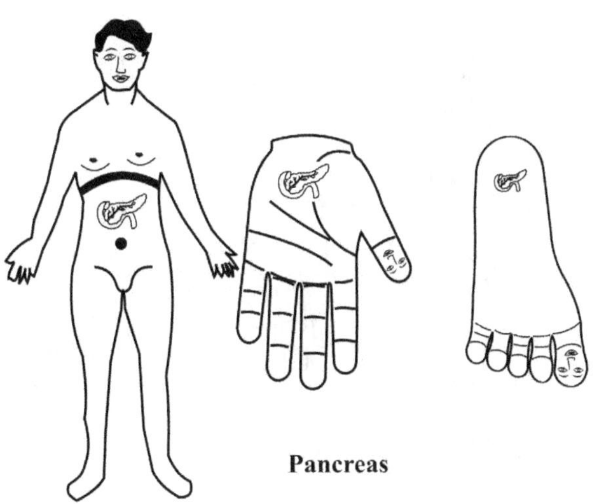

Pancreas

Pancreas (Fig 29)

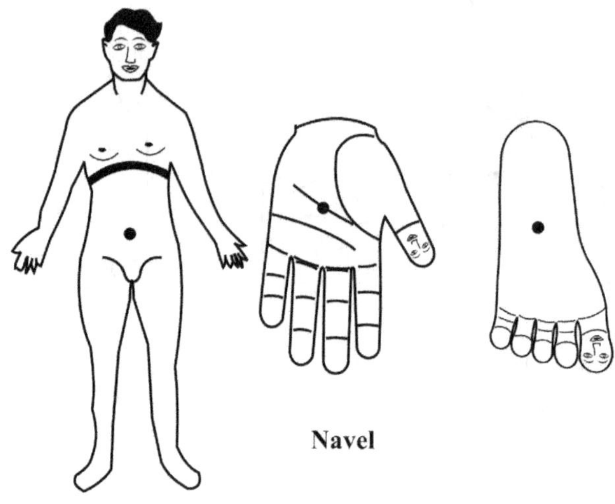

Navel

Naval (Fig. 30)

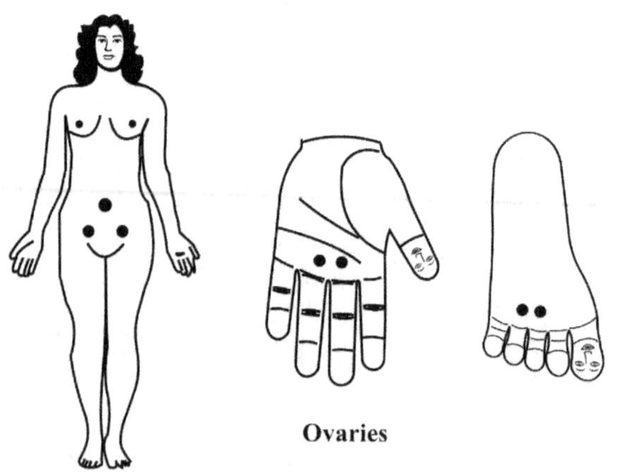

Ovaries

Ovaries (Fig. 31)

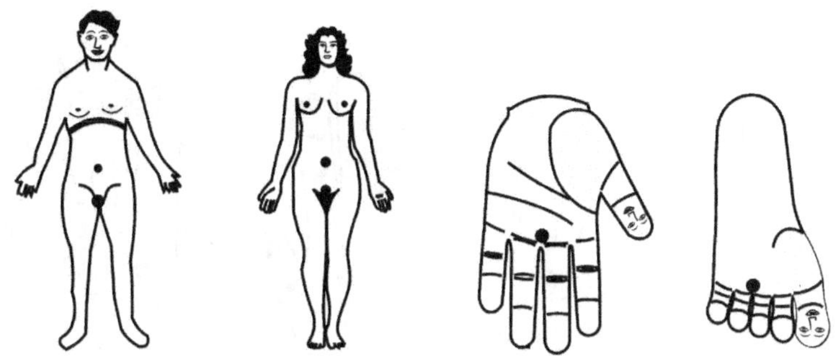

Vagina /Uterus / Prostate / Urinary / Bladder (Fig 32)

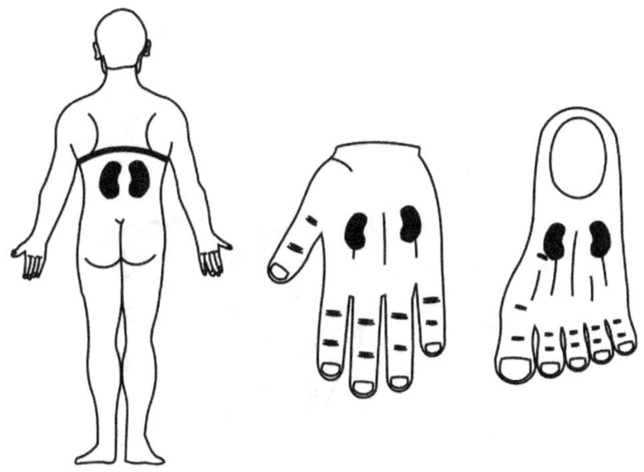

Kidneys (Fig. 33)

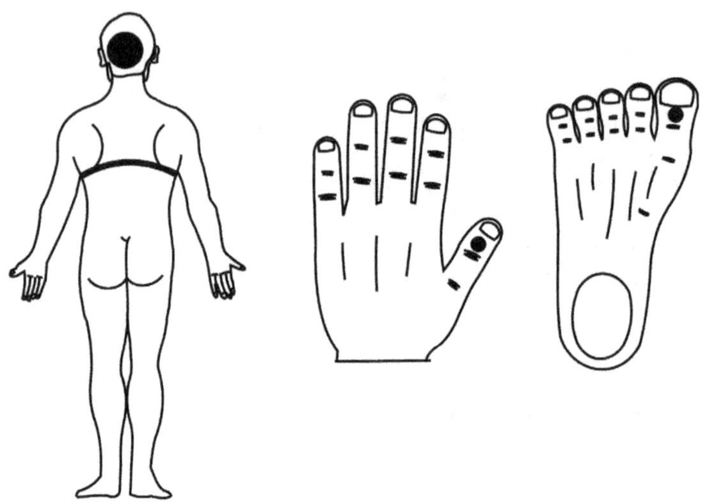

Occipital Area (Fig. 34)

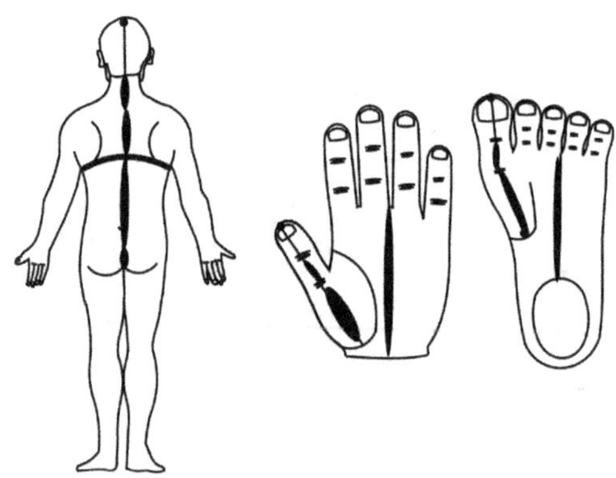

Spinal Cord (Fig. 35)

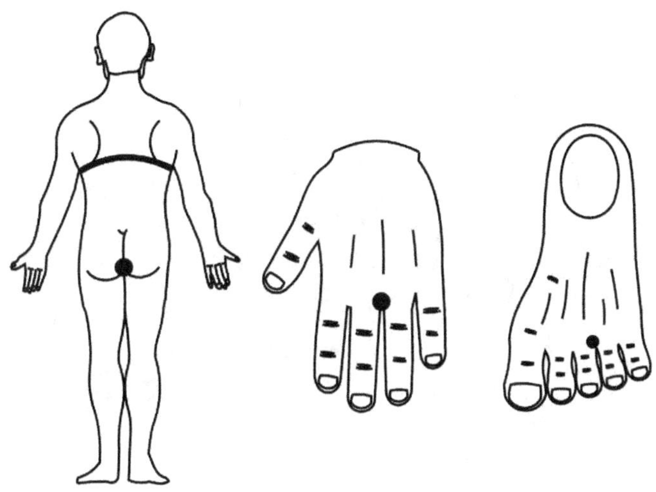

Anus (Fig. 36)

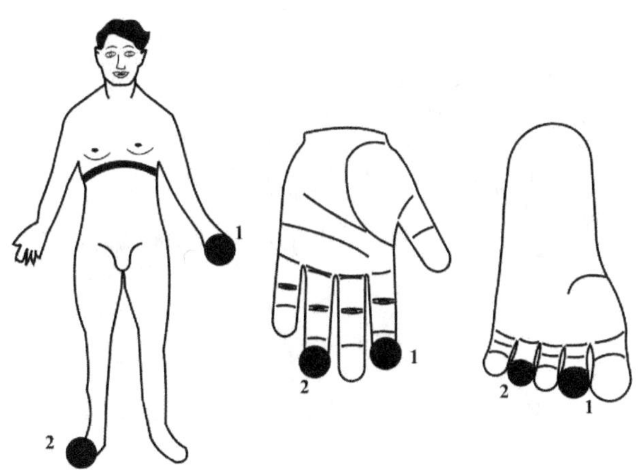

Left Hand and Right Foot (Fig. 37)

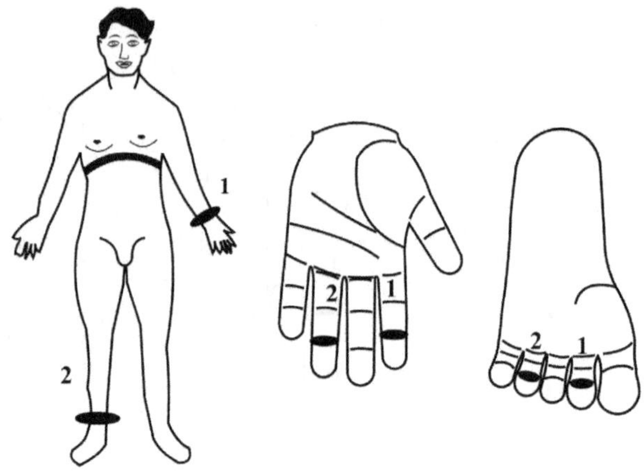

Right Ankle and Left Wrist Joint (Fig. 38)

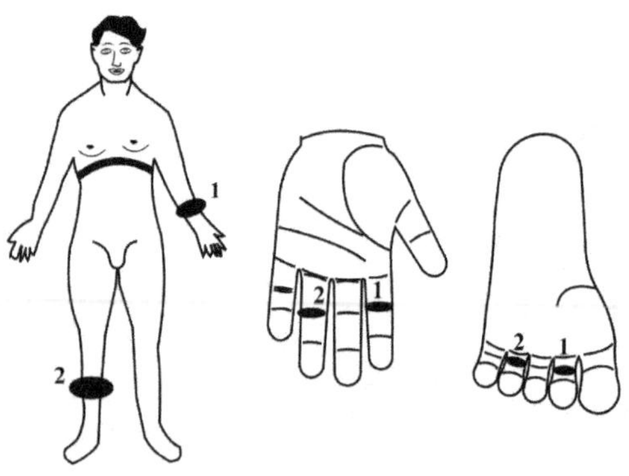

Right Knee and Left Elbow (Fig. 39)

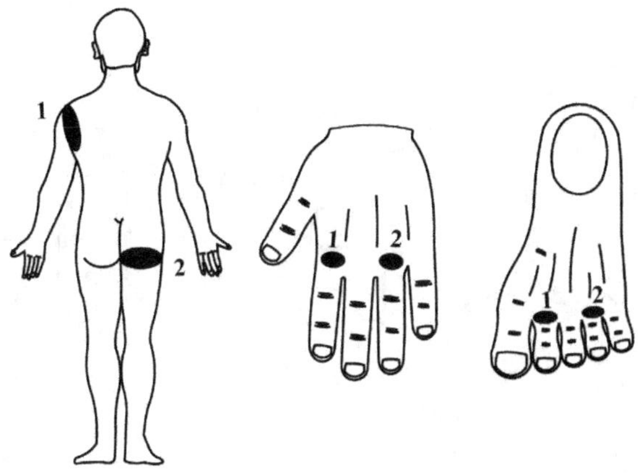

Left Shoulder and Right Hip Joint (Fig. 40)

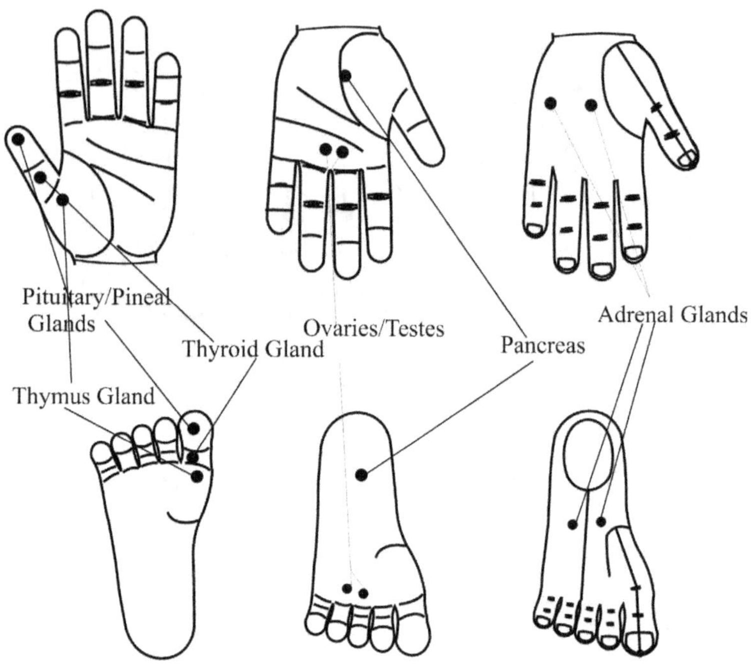

Endocrine Glands (Fig. 41)

Although it is not in the scope of this course, yet I have given an idea of functions of various endocrine glands in the end of this lesson.

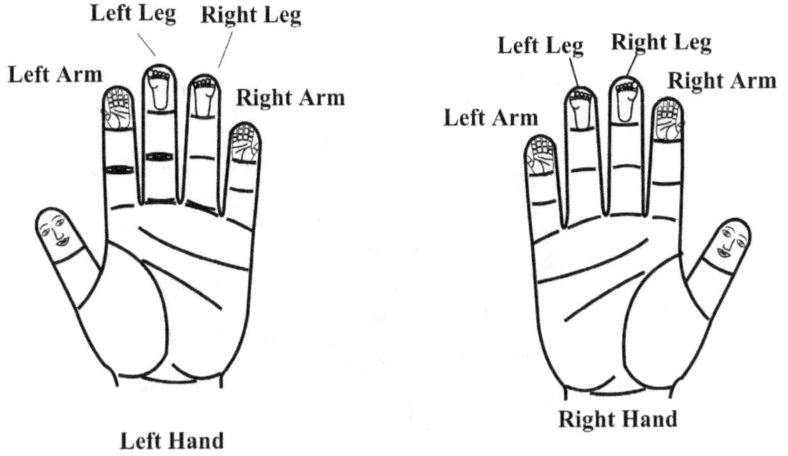

Arms/Legs : Yin (Fig. 42)

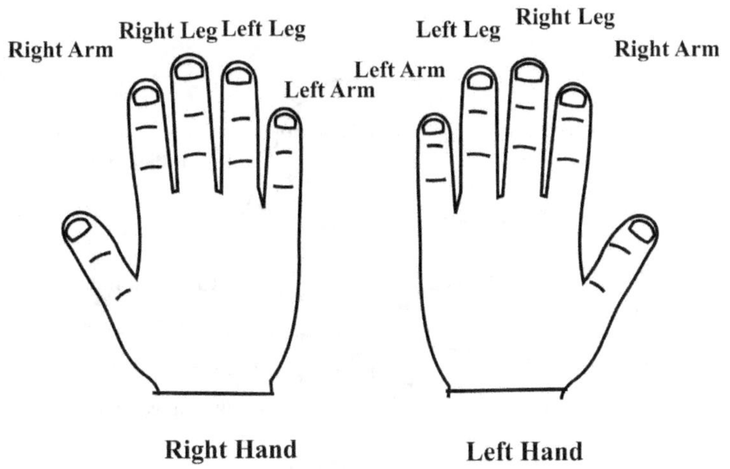

Arm/Legs (Yang) Fig 42a

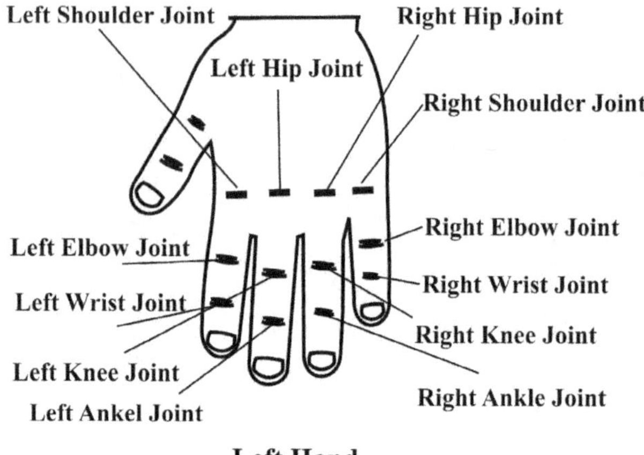

Joints : Left Hand (Fig. 43)

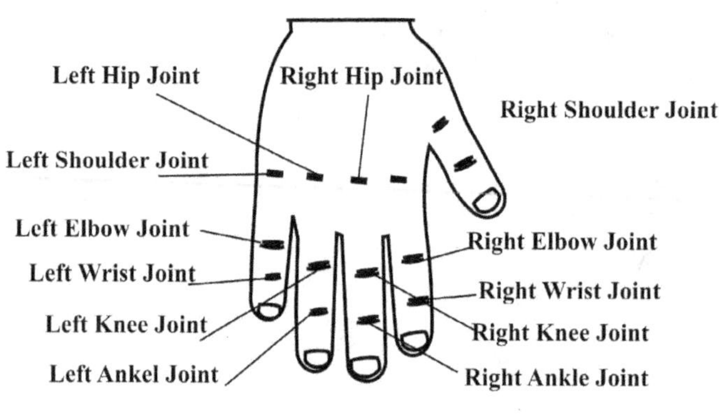

Fig. 43a : Right Hand

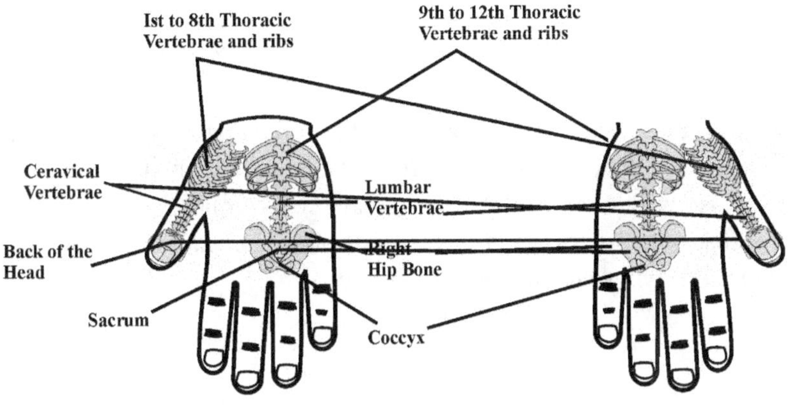

Spinal Cord Hands (Fig. 44A)

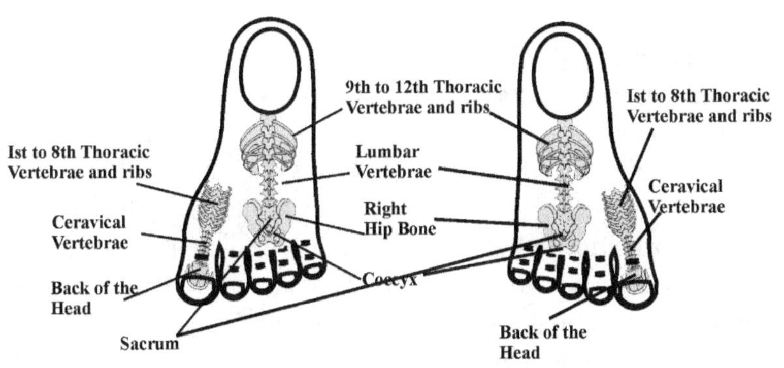

Spinal Cord Feet (Fig 44b)

Endocrine Gland System : Your endocrine system includes all the glands in your body that make hormones. These chemical messengers play a key role in making sure your body works the way it should.

If your endocrine system isn't healthy, you might have problems developing during puberty, getting pregnant, or managing stress. You also might gain weight easily, have weak bones, or lack energy because too much sugar stays in your blood instead of moving into your cells where it's needed for energy.

Key Parts

Many different glands make up the endocrine system. The hypothalamus, pituitary gland, and pineal gland are your brain. The thyroid and parathyroid glands are in your neck. The thymus is between your lungs, the adrenals are on top of your kidneys, and the pancreas is behind your stomach. Your ovaries (if you're a woman) or testes (if you're a man) are in your pelvic region.

Hypothalamus: This organ connects your endocrine system with your nervous system. Its main job is to tell your pituitary gland to start or stop making hormones.

Pituitary: This is the "master" gland of your endocrine system. It uses information it gets from your brain to "tell" other glands in your body what to do. It makes many different important hormones, including growth hormone; prolactin, which helps breastfeeding moms make milk; and luteinizing hormone, which manages estrogen in women and testosterone in men.

Pineal: This gland makes a chemical called melatonin. It helps your body get ready to go to sleep.

Thyroid: This gland makes thyroid hormone, which controls your metabolism. If this gland doesn't make enough (a condition called hypothyroidism), everything happens more slowly. Your heart rate might slow down. You could get constipated. And you might gain weight. If it makes too much (hyperthyroidism), everything speeds up. Your heart might race. You could have diarrhea. And you might lose weight without trying.

Parathyroid: This is a set of four small glands behind your thyroid. They are important for bone health. The glands control your levels of calcium and phosphorus.

Thymus: This gland makes white blood cells called T-lymphocytes that fight infection and are crucial as a child's immune system develops. The thymus starts to shrink after puberty.

Adrenals: Best known for making the "fight or flight" hormone adrenaline (epinephrine), these two glands also make corticosteroids. These are hormones that affect your metabolism and sexual function, among other things.

Pancreas: The pancreas is part of both your digestive and endocrine systems. It makes digestive enzymes that break down food. It also makes the hormones insulin and glucagon. These help ensure you have the right amount of sugar in your bloodstream and your cells.

If you don't make any insulin, which is the case for people with type 1 diabetes, your blood sugar levels can get dangerously high. In type 2 diabetes, the pancreas usually makes some insulin but not enough.

Ovaries: In women, these organs make estrogen and progesterone. These hormones help develop breasts at puberty, regulate the menstrual cycle, and support a pregnancy.

Testes: In men, the testes make testosterone. It helps them grow facial and body hair at puberty. It also tells the penis to grow larger and plays a role in making sperm.

CHAPTER THREE

LOCATING EXACT CORRESPONDENCE POINTS

After having gone through the correspondence points for various body organs in general, it is important to understand the exact location of the correspondence points. Following paras will help understand the location of the exact correspondence points.

A. Correspondence Points in relation to Reference Lines :

It is easy to understand the correspondence points in relation to two reference lines: Diaphragm Line and Centre Line.

i. Correspondence Points in relation to Diaphragm Line :

Diaphragm is a muscular membrane dividing chest and abdomen in the body. In the body, chest, lungs, heart, and face, etc. are above the diaphragm and abdominal organs are below the diaphragm. Now we have to understand the correspondence Diaphragm Line. Once this is understood, location of the correspondence points becomes easier.

The only thing to understand in relation to diaphragm line is that there are two correspondence diaphragm lines on the palms or soles, whereas there is only one diaphragm in the body. One correspondence diaphragm line is below the thumb, where the chest portion ends, and the other correspondence diaphragm line is at the end of the hand/foot, i.e. the wrist line on the palm or the heel line of the sole.

When finding a correspondence point to a part above the diaphragm line in the Yin area of the hand/foot, the diaphragm corresponds to the line below the thumb, as shown in Fig. 45.

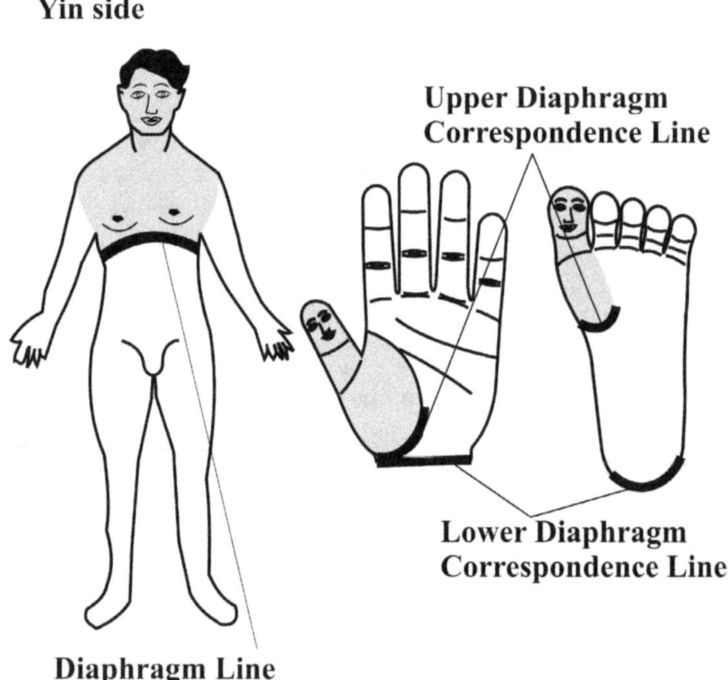

Fig. 45

When finding a correspondence point to a part above the diaphragm line in the Yang area of the hand/foot, the diaphragm corresponds to the line below the thumb, as shown in Fig. 46.

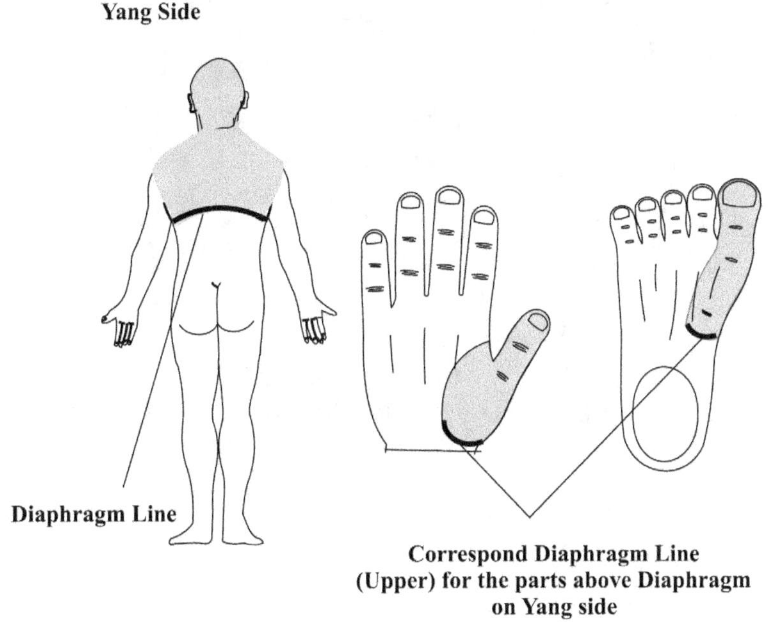

Fig. 46

When finding a correspondence point to a part below the diaphragm line in the Yin area of the hand/foot, the diaphragm corresponds to the base of the palm /heel, as shown in Fig. 47.

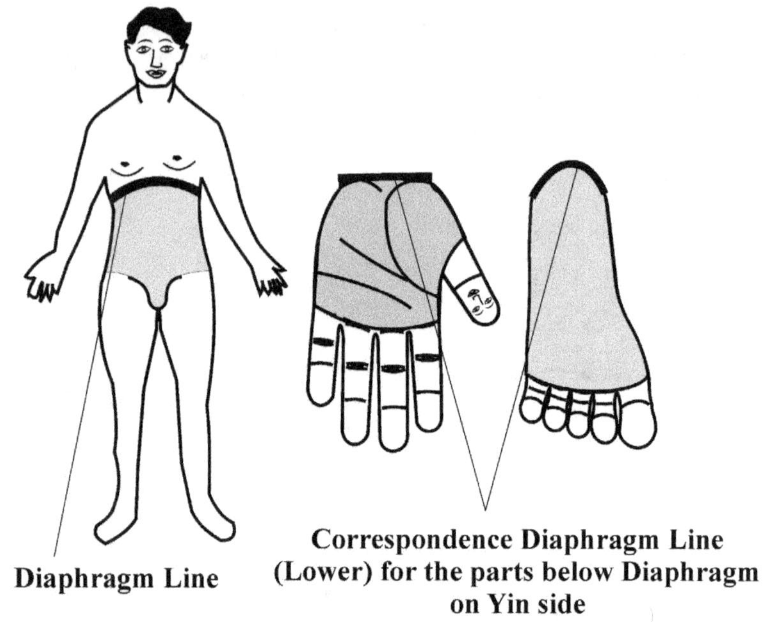

Fig. 47

When finding a correspondence point to a part below the diaphragm line in the Yang area of the hand/foot, the diaphragm corresponds to the base palm line and base heel line, i.e. end of the hand/foot, as shown in Fig. 48.

In order to locate the correspondence points above the Diaphragm line, one must keep the hand so that its thumb would face up and to locate correspondence points below the diaphragm line, one must keep the hands with all fingers pointing downward.

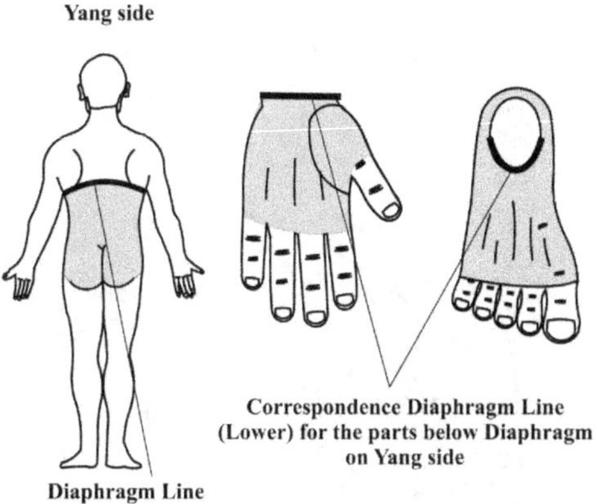

Fig. 48

Now let us understand the position of internal organs of the body and their correspondence points in hands / feet in relation to Diaphragm Line.

Above Diaphragm : Face, Lungs, and Heart (Fig. 49)

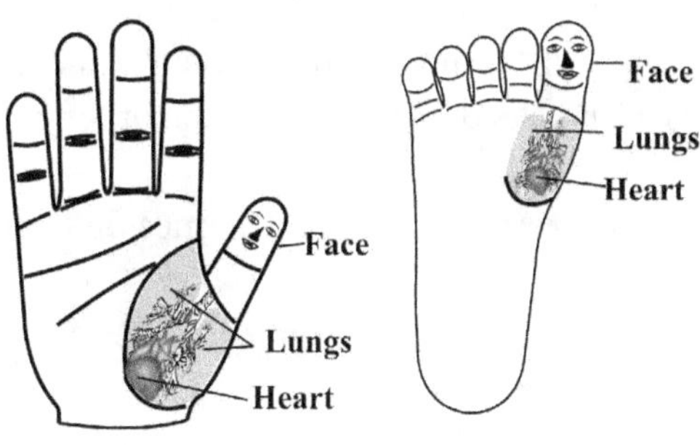

Fig. 49

Below Diaphragm : Liver, Gall Bladder, Stomach, Large Intestine, Small Intestine (Fig. 50)

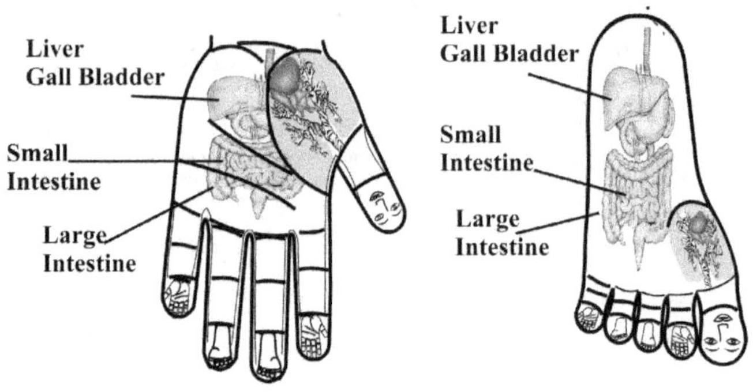

Fig. 50

ii. Correspondence Centreline

Centreline is an imaginary line drawn vertically in the body, with one end at the Head Top and the other end at the Genital Organs point, passing through Stomach Pit on the Yin side. On the Yang side, one end is at the Head Top, whereas the other end is the Anus.

But there are two correspondence centre lines on hands/feet.

First Correspondence Centre Line on Yin side : Above Diaphragm Line.

One point for the first correspondence centre line of the Yin side of the hand is at the genital organs correspondence point where the middle finger and the ring finger meet together, and the other point is the Yin centre of the upper Diaphragm Line. Fig 51

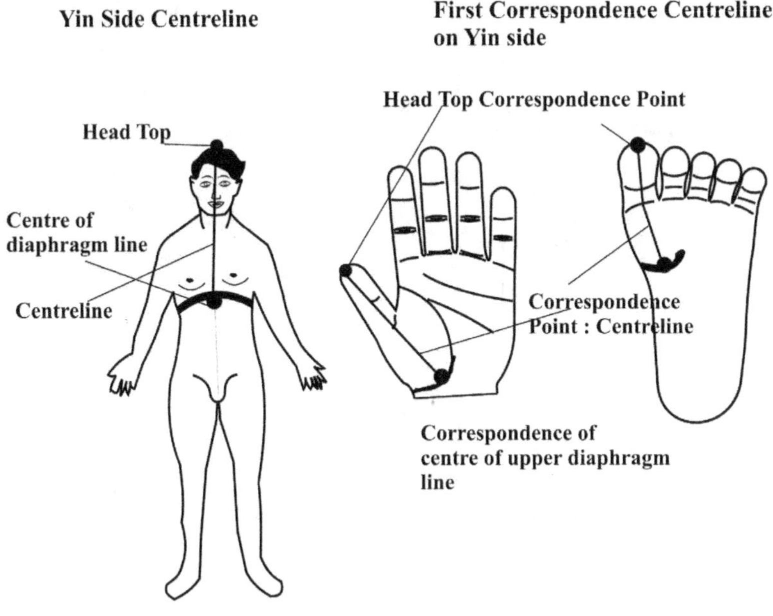

Fig. 51

Second Correspondence Centre Line : Yin side : Below Diaphragm Line

One point for the second correspondence centre line of the Yin side of the hand is at the Head Top correspondence point in the centre of the thumb and the other point is at the centre of the base of the thumb, i.e. centre of the lower Diaphragm Line. (Fig. 52)

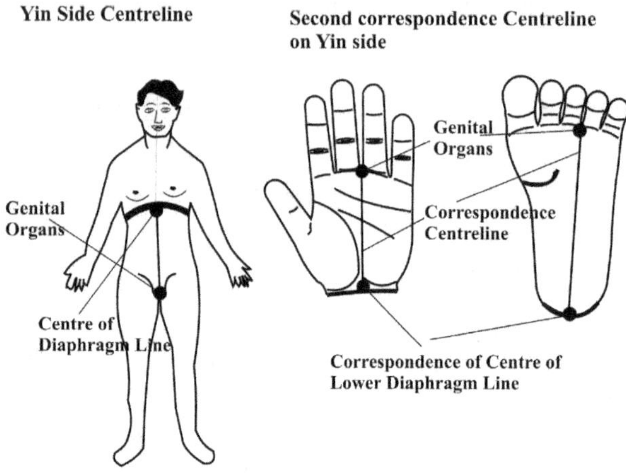

Fig. 52

First Correspondence Centre Line : Yang side : Above Diaphragm Line

One point for the second correspondence centre line is at the correspondence point of Head Top in the centre of the thumb and the other point is at the centre of the base of the thumb, i.e. centre of the lower Diaphragm Line. (Fig. 53A)

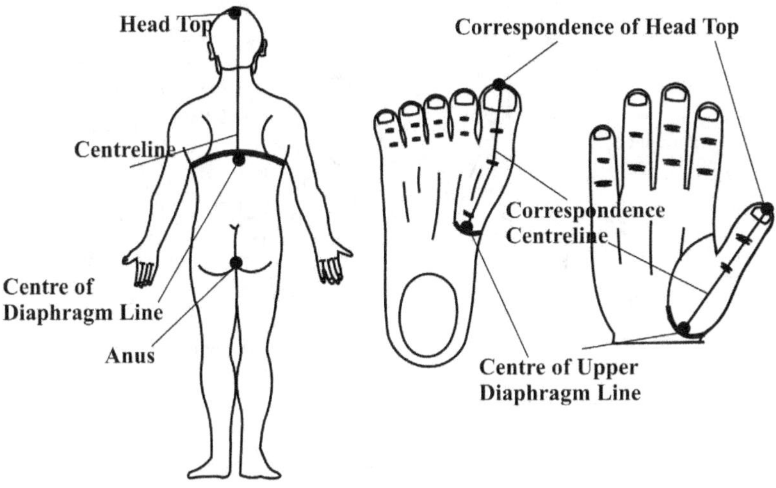

Fig. 53A

Second Correspondence Centre Line : Yang side : Below Diaphragm Line

For the Yang side, one point for the first correspondence centre line is at the anus correspondence point where the middle finger and the ring finger meet together, and the other point is at the centre of the base wrist line (Fig 53B)

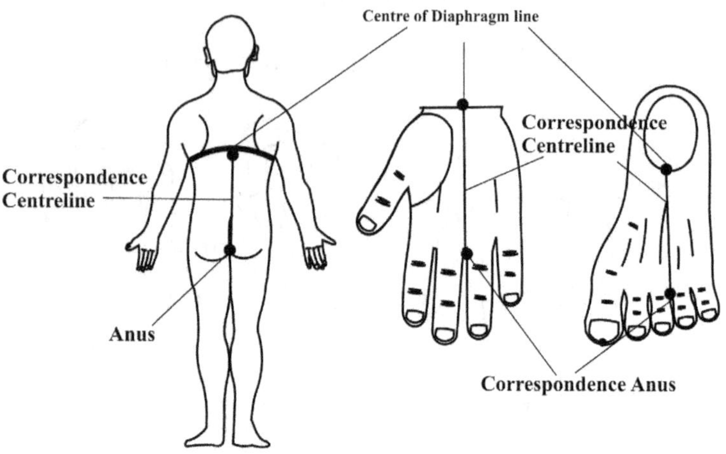

Fig. 53B

Similarly, the correspondence centre lines of the Yin and Yang sides of the foot can be understood.

B. UNDERSTANDING LEFT AND RIGHT PARTS OF THE BODY

Yet another feature which confuses the mind so often is the left-right concept of the correspondence points. Following figures (No. 54 and 55 and Fig 55 and 56) would help understand this concept more clearly.

Above Diaphragm Points

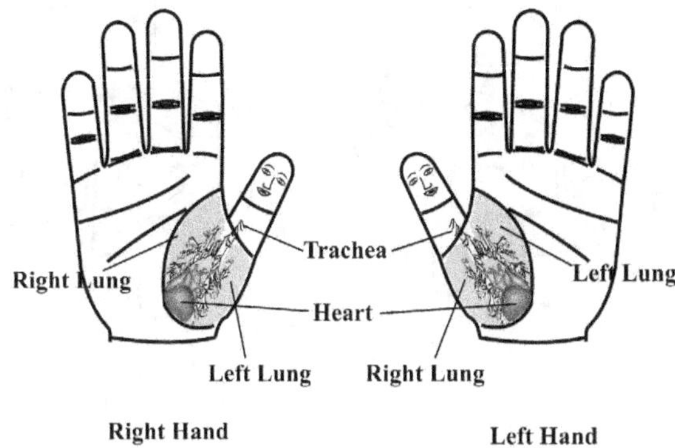

Fig. 54 and Fig. 55

Below Diaphragm Points (Fig. 57 and Fig 57A)

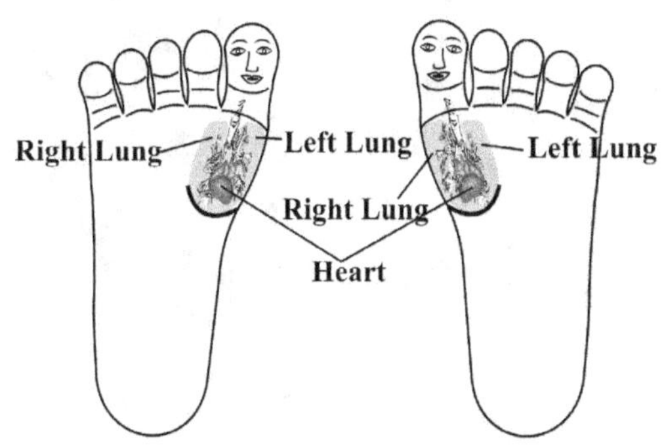

Fig. 56

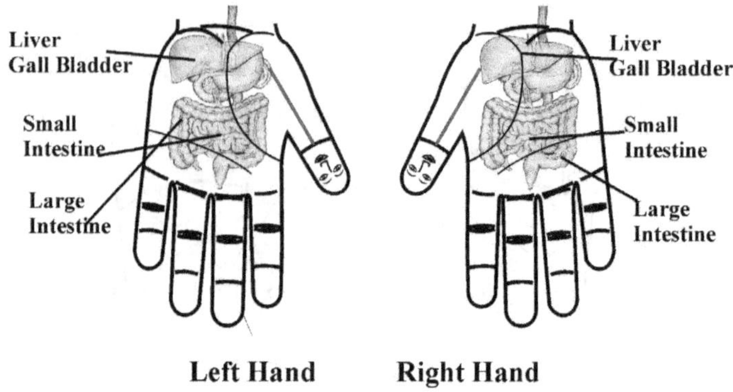

Fig. 57

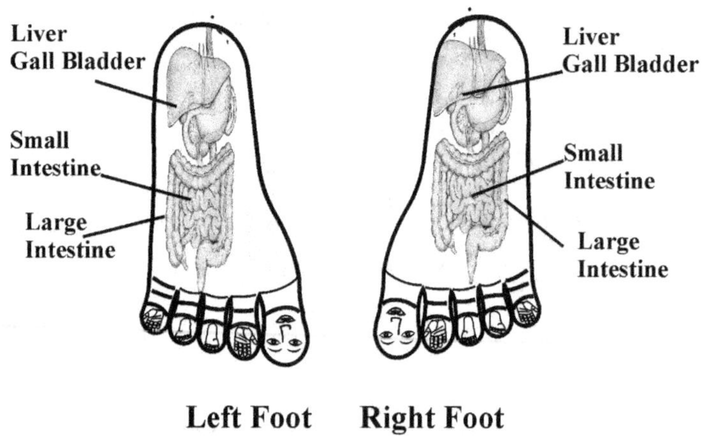

Fig. 57A

C. Primary and Secondary Correspondence points :

In the usual Acupressure/Reflexology system, one body is
represented in two hands or two feet. As there is one Liver in the

body on the right side, there is one point for Liver in the right hand, and so on.

But in the SuJok Therapy, it is not so. Complete body is mapped on one hand or one foot. Hence, we have got two bodies on our hands, i.e. one in each hand. Therefore, there will be two Liver points; one in each hand. It is, therefore, necessary to distinguish between these two points. In addition, two bodies will be available in the feet also.

If the body organ is on the right side of the body, then its correspondence point on the right hand/foot is called the Primary Correspondence point and its correspondence point on the left hand is called the Secondary Correspondence Point.

Since the Appendix in the body (Fig 58) exist in the right part of the body, its Primary Correspondence Point (Fig 59) will be in the right part of the right hand/foot, whereas its Secondary Correspondence Point (Fig 60) will be in the right part of the left hand/foot, as shown below : **Fig. 58**

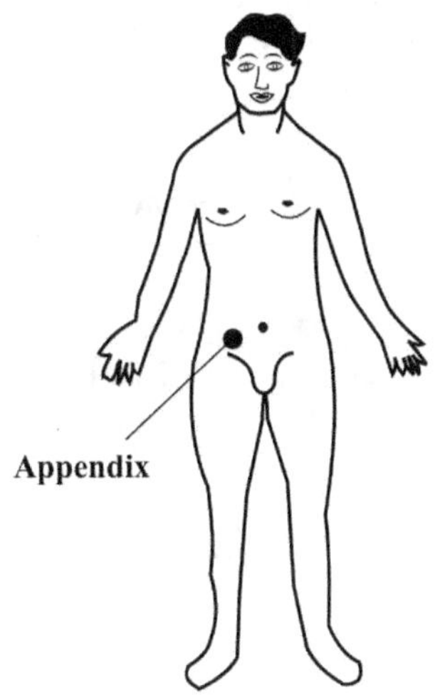

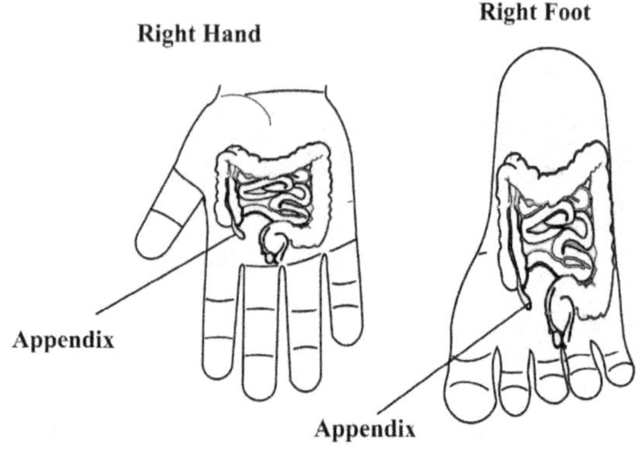

**Appendix : Primary Response Point
on Right Hand and Right Foot**

Fig. 59

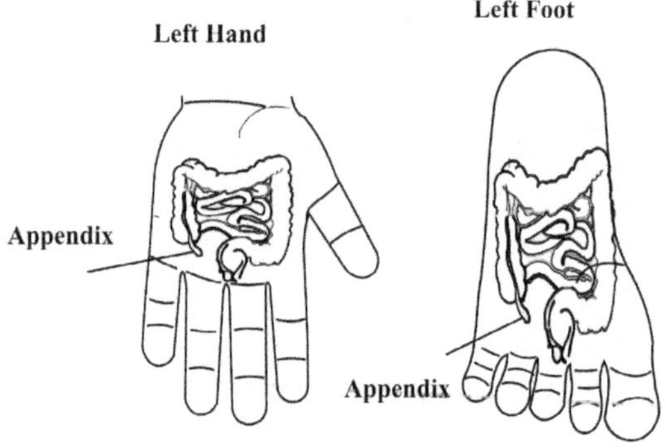

**Appendix : Secondary Correspondence Point
on Right Hand and Right Foot**

Fig. 60

Similarly, a distinction can be made in other cases. For example, let us take the Left Ear in the body (Fig 61). The Primary Correspondence Point for the Left Ear will be in the left hand/ foot (Fig. 62) and the Secondary Correspondence Point in the right hand / right foot (Fig 63) , as shown below :

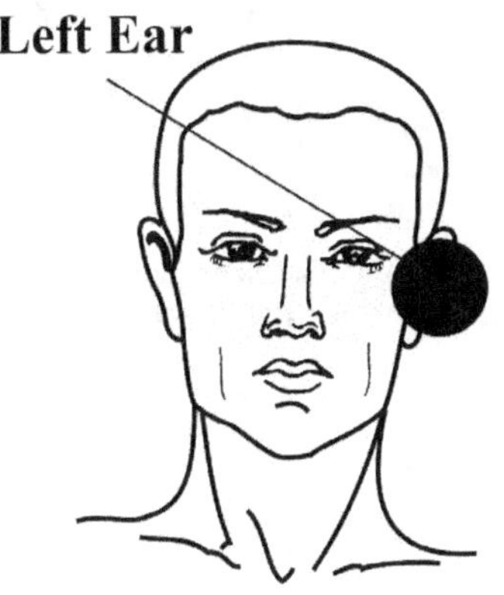

Fig. 61

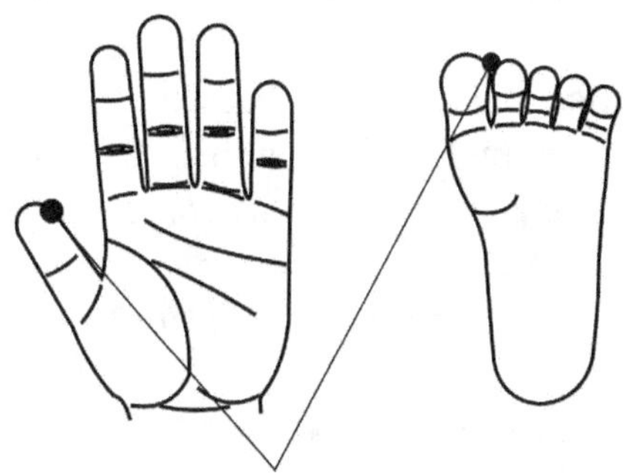

Primary Correspondence Point :
Left Ear : Left Hand / LeftFoot

Fig. 62

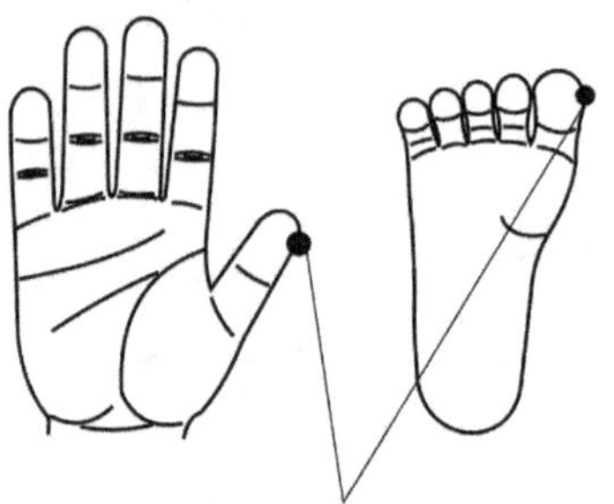

Secondary Correspondence Point :
Left Ear : Right Hand / Right Foot

Fig. 63

In order to cure diseases, it is required to check both of the correspondence points and select a point with the stronger pain reaction as the cure point or treat both the points.

D. Correspondence Points in relation to Yin and Yang points:

It is being mentioned here again because it is a very important concept. Understanding the difference between Yin or Yang organs/parts will help locate the exact correspondence points.

Also Refer to Lesson 1 and Figs. 14A and 14B

a. Yin and Yang on legs :

Since there is a slight deviation in the yin-yang of the body and yin-yang of the leg structure, this aspect is being explained here.

Seen from the front, the inside of the Leg is Yin and the outside is Yang. The centre line passing through the front knee will be the Yin-Yang border. (Fig 64.)

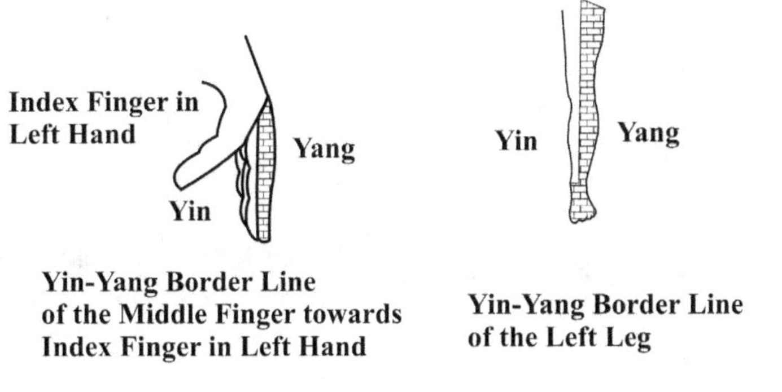

Fig. 64

The elbow joint is bent towards the Yin area. Likewise, its correspondence, the 2nd knuckle of the Index Finger, is bent towards the Yin area.

On the other hand, the knee joint is bent with Yin and Yang mixed half and half, but its correspondence, the Middle Finger, is bent towards the Yin area only.

In other words, there are two centre lines in the Middle Finger, where the Yin and Yang sides meet together. In the right hand, the line facing the 2nd finger is the front knee and the line facing the 3th finger is the rear knee. (Fig. 65)

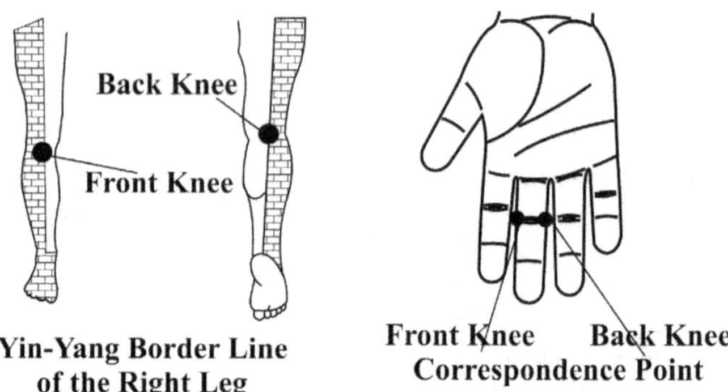

Fig. 65

Yin and Yang of Foot: Fig. 65a

It is easy to understand the Yin-Yang division on the hand, but it is slightly difficult on the foot. Down to the ankle it is easy to tell the difference between the Yin and Yang areas under the Yin-Yang principles just as in the leg.

Below the ankle, however, the instep becomes the Yang area and the sole becomes the Yin area, i.e. the angle of Yin and Yang areas are about 90° turned inside. But in its correspondence area of the middle finger, the Yin and Yang correspondence areas of foot are kept continued without change of angle.Fig 65a

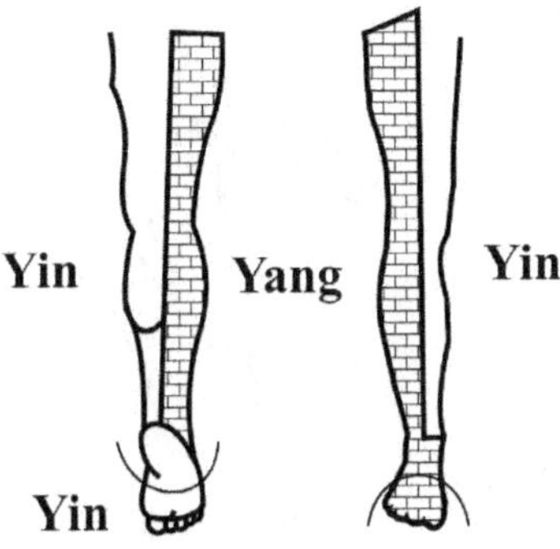

Fig. 65A

E. Understanding flanks (side surfaces) of the body:

The Correspondence Points for flanks are located on the Yin-Yang borders of the hands and feet. It is easy to locate the exact points on the Yin-Yang borders for flanks, except the Primary Correspondence points for the flank on the thoracic cavity. This difficulty arises because of the thumb's position in the hand, as it is not exactly like the head of the body. As said earlier, for this we have to imagine as if the thumb is removed from the side of the fingers and placed on the top of the palm, as shown in Lesson 1.

However, for the sake of clear understanding, following figures are given: **Fig 66**

For Flanks above Diaphragm Line

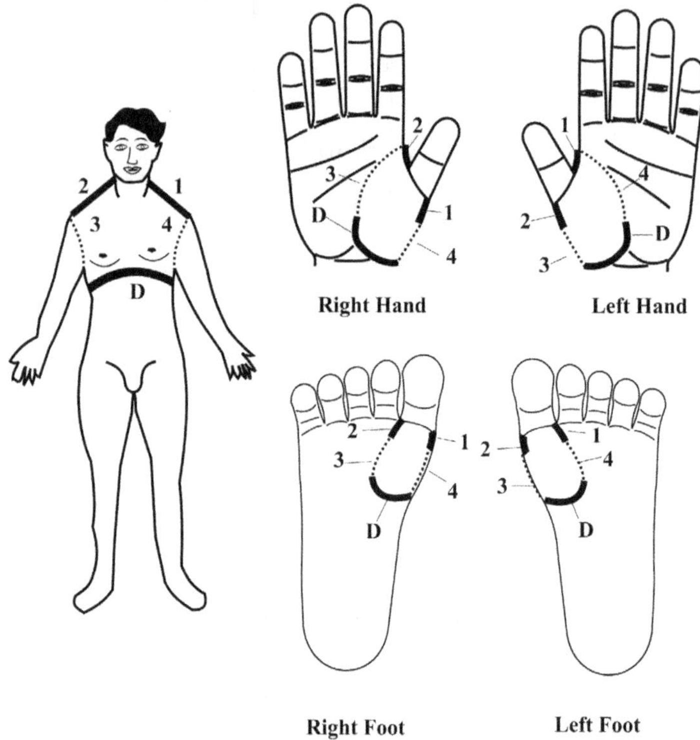

Fig. 66

For flanks below Diaphragm Line
Right Hand
Left Hand
2
D
1
2
1
2
2
1
Right Foot
Left Foot
D
2
2
1

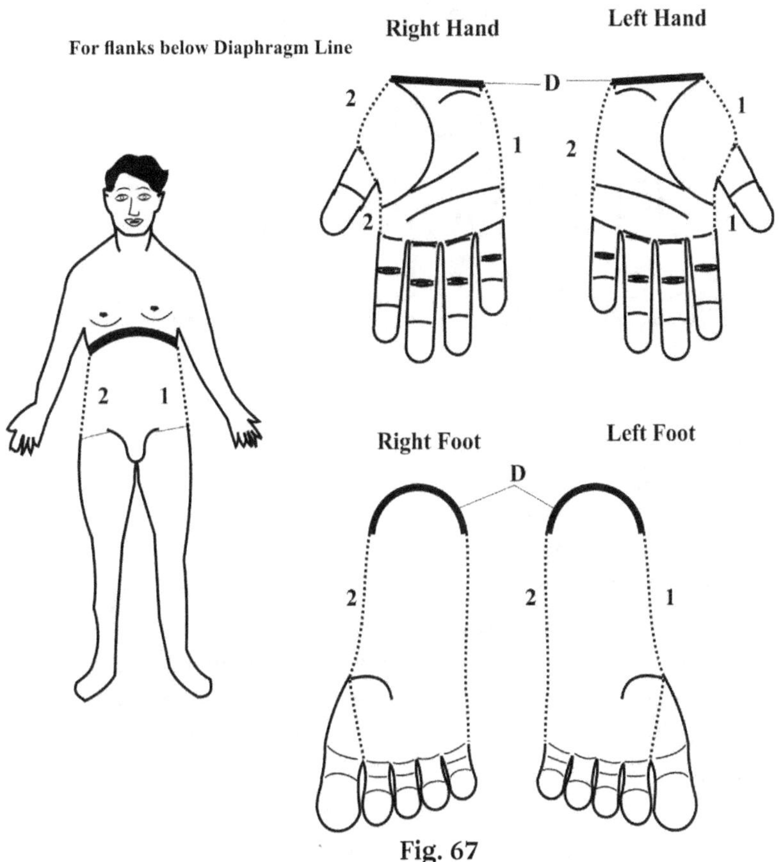

Fig. 67

CHAPTER FOUR

PRESSURE AND MASSAGE TECHNIQUES

A point which responds to a disease or malfunctioning of an organ/ part of the body is called the Correspondence Point for that organ/ part of the body. In simple words, it means that when a particular organ of the body is diseased/unhealthy, its correspondence point in hand or foot would become tender and show increase in pain on being touched or it shows discolouring of the skin or swelling. If this point is treated/stimulated by pressure through any means, its tenderness goes away and pain disappears, restoring health to that organ/part of the body, to which it corresponds. This is called a Correspondence System.

We are all aware that there is energy flow in our body, e.g. electromagnetic waves. If this energy flow is disturbed, the concerned part becomes sick. Through the correspondence system, this disturbance is felt in the correspondence points in the form of globules or balls. These balls are highly sensitive to external influences and are very painful to press. Natural or artificial stimulation of correspondence areas starts curative electromagnetic waves that travel backwards to the sick part and normalises the energy state of this area.

In order to give effective help, it is necessary to locate the correspondence point (or the correspondence globule or ball) for the diseased part. Using the principles explained in the previous Chapters, one can find the exact location of the treatment point.

How to locate the Correspondence Point :

First of all find out the diseased body part.

1. Then find out whether the diseased body part is on Yang or Yin surface of the body.
2. Then also find out the correspondence point in relation to Diaphragm Line and Centre Line.
3. Then also find out whether the diseased part is some kind of a Joint. If yes, which joint? If the parts in some bony part, little more pressure has to be given to get the reaction from the patient.
4. Keeping the above in mind, locate the correspondence part in hand or foot.
    Now give pressure on the located correspondence point. If this is the correct correspondence point, the patient will feel pain and will withdraw his hand. Then you can be sure that this is the correct correspondence point.Now massage the correspondence point with fingers or use seeds on them.
5. Then you can also keep in mind the primary and secondary correspondence point for this diseased that correspondence part which results into more pain. It could be primary or secondary correspondence point.

See following Fig. No. 68. Keeping the above in mind, the correspondence part of the diseased body part has been located.

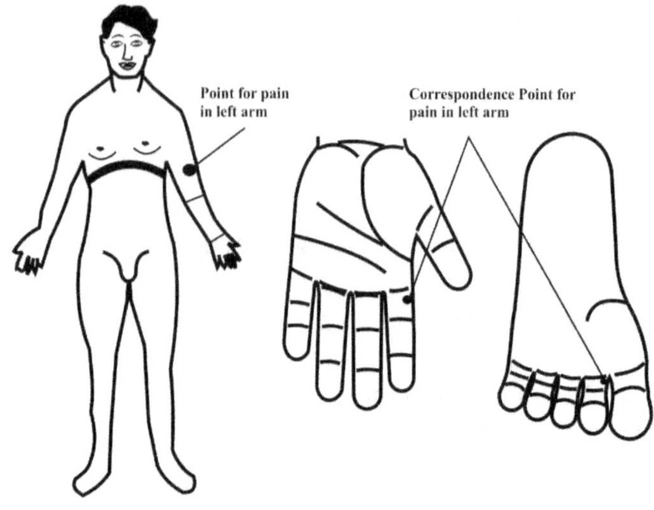

Fig. 68

Methods of treatment

Many gadgets or instruments are used in Sujok Therapy treatment. In Sujok therapy usually we check whether is hyperactive or hypoactive. If it is hyperactive, we sedate this point, i.e. we decrease energy thereon. If a correspondence hurts on putting a pressure on it, it is called hyperactive. And if a correspondence points feels relief on putting a pressure on it, it is hypoactive. It is a general rule. If you know the functions of organs, then also you can guess which is overactive and which is underactive. And if it is hypoactive, we tonify this point, i.e. we increase the energy on this point. Usually we do this with magnets on correspondence points. But for Seed Therapy, we just affix a seed on it and the energy of seed will balance the energy on that point. More methods of Seed Therapy are given in latter chapters.

I am not mentioning Sujok methods and gadgets here because this book is on Sujok Seed Healing.

Hence I am mentioning below the pressure/massage and seeds methods. (To know about Sujok Correspondence Points locations and gadgets, read our books Sujok Correspondence Points and Sujok Therapy).

Having located the exact correspondence point, give pressure on this point with fingers or thumb. You can do massage also.

I. Pressure :

i. Give pressure on the correspondence point with the fingers or thumb. Pressure should be so much that the patient feels some pain and is able to give pain reaction, i.e. he withdraws his hand. The pressure should not be so much that the patient cries with pain or should not be so little that the patient does not respond.

ii. Choosing the right amount of pressure also depends upon the location of the correspondence point. If the correspondence point is in some bony part, i.e. a joint, a little more amount of pressure is required. If the correspondence point is in skin, then lot of pressure is not required.

iii. Give pressure for a second or two, hold the finger/thumb there for a second or two, then again press. Continue this on-off pressure technique. You can give pressure for 10 or so minutes and then stop.

II. Massage :

The Correspondence points can be stimulated by massaging. As a result of this massage, there may be reddening of the skin being massaged or there may he feeling of warmth in that area.

Pressure/Massage techniques

i. Interrupted Pressure : In this technique strong pressing movements are made with one or several fingers as well as with finger joints. This manipulation can be performed with both hands. (Fig 69)

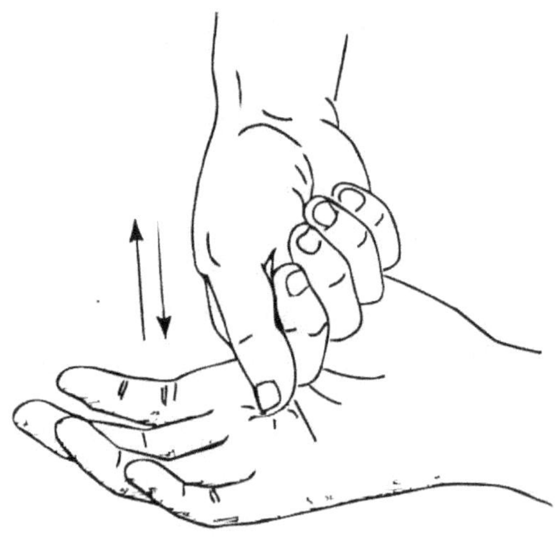

Fig. 69

ii. Pinching : In this technique, the skin and subcutaneous tissues are pinched with the first and second fingers till the persistent reddening appears. This manipulation is done by strong pressure. Pinching is effective for stimulation of the heart and lungs correspondence areas. (Fig 70)

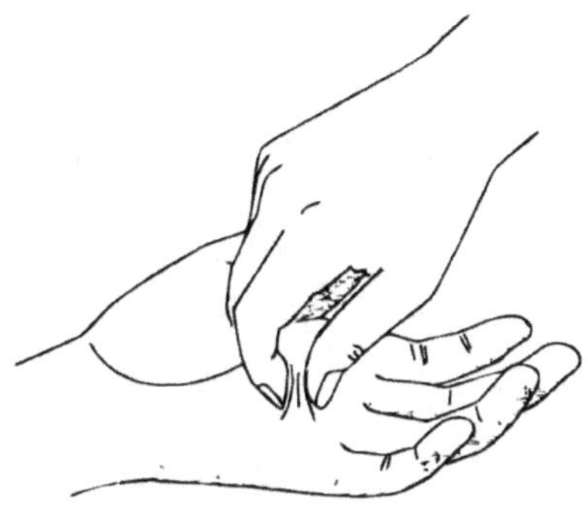

Fig. 70

iii. Rubbing : is performed with one or two fingers. Rubbing movements should be very intensive. It is especially convenient to rub the Head correspondence areas as located on the tips of fingers and toes. (Fig 71)

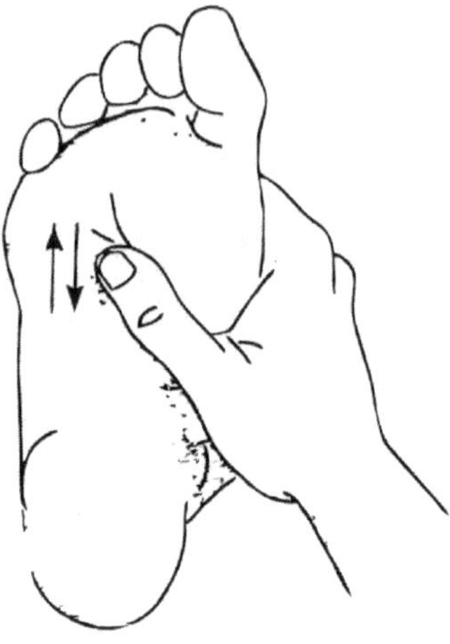

Fig. 71

iv. Vibration : In this technique, the correspondence point is acted upon by strong vibration movements of the fingers. The frequency is 160-180 vibrations per minute.

v. Linear massage : is performed with fingers, and in a definite direction depending on the character of affliction. For example, in case of difficult inhalation the linear massage is carried out in the direction corresponding to that of the air coming and passing through the respiratory tracts. (Fig 72)

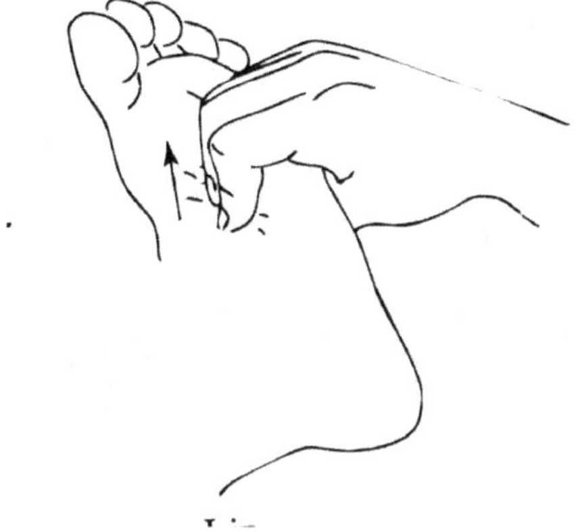

Fig. 72

vi. Rotational massage : is carried out by circular movement of the one or several fingers in the region of a correspondence area with the frequency of about 60 rotations per minute. This manipulation is also performed with substantial pressing effort. (Fig 73)

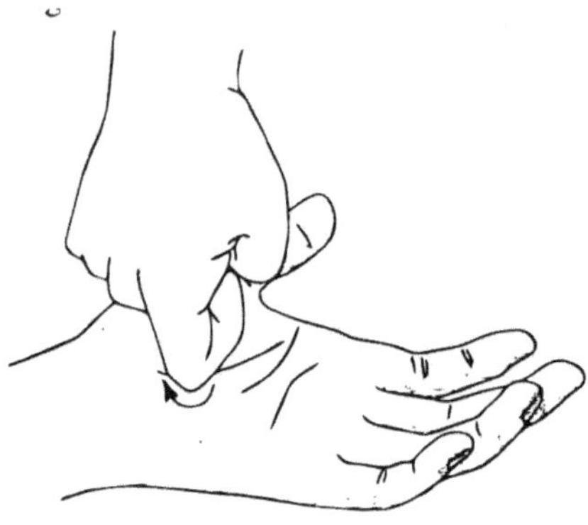

Fig. 73

Precautions in Treatment :

i. Do not give a very strong stimulation / pressure to a weak patient.
ii. In case the patient is under tension or stress, do not give stimulation.
iii. Do not give a strong stimulus when a patient has not slept well or starved.
iv. Do not give too strong stimulus on the correspondence point to the head.
v. Do not give a strong stimulus to a patient who is afraid of treatment.
vi. Do not give a strong stimulus to children, pregnant ladies, or old men.

Number of Applications and Duration of Treatment:

The number and duration of treatment differ depending on whether the disease is serious or not, patient's condition, the method and techniques used, etc.

CHAPTER FIVE

BASIC TREATMENT METHODS

For most of the simple or acute diseases, a simple stimulation of the concerned correspondence point on hand/foot results in restoration of health. However, the stimulation of only one point of correspondence does not give a desirable result in all cases, especially in chronic cases. One has always to find more correspondence points involved for a particular disease. For example, for acidity, the correspondence point for liver only would not suffice. It would be judicious to apply stimulation on the various points pertaining to digestive system. Also, it is necessary to find out all the painful points in the supposed area of correspondence. If even after stimulating with sufficient force the concerned correspondence points, the patient is not completely relieved of pain, it means that there are still other points of correspondence which should be additionally stimulated.

Treatment Methods : Theare a number of methods for treatment :

Seed Therapy Through One Point : Gall Bladder Problem

One-Point Simple Stimulation of the relevant Correspondence Point. For Gall Bladder problem. Affix a seed on the relevant point.(Fig. 74)

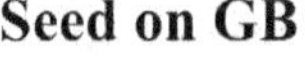

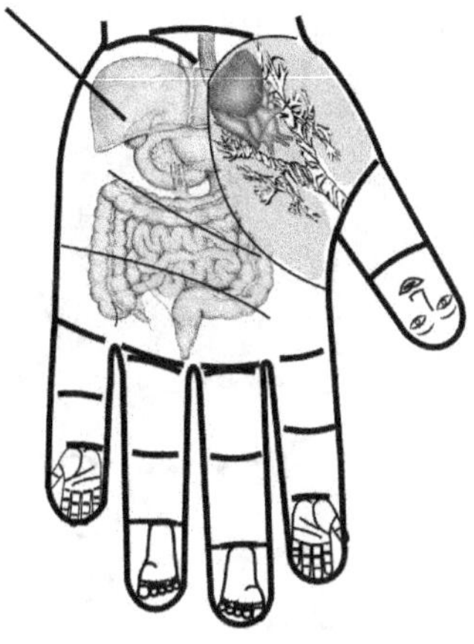

Fig. 74

Seed Therapy Through Two Points
Liver Problem

If the diseased area is more and it is difficult to pinpoint the exact point, this method is utilised. In order to avoid stimulation of all points of correspondence in this area, only two points limiting the sick part are stimulated. More often than not, it is sufficient to treat these two points for the pain in the correspondence area between them to restore health to the diseased area. The figure shows two seeds on the Liver Area for Liver pain. Affix two seeds one each on the points as shown in Fig. 75.

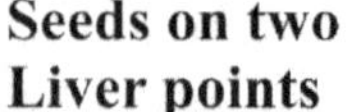

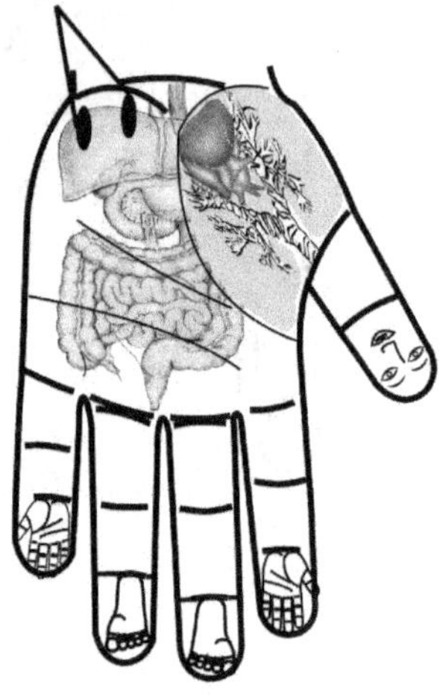

Fig. 75

In short, if the affected region is large, the number of corresponding points increases. In this case only two points may be stimulated, restricting the affected area. If the affected area is of oblong shape (spine, extremities), then the initial and terminating points are used. If an internal organ is influenced, the points corresponding to the top and bottom or left and right borders of the organ are used. Picture (Fig. 76) below shows the use of seeds for pains in the thoracic spine through two-point system as per Standard Correspondence System.

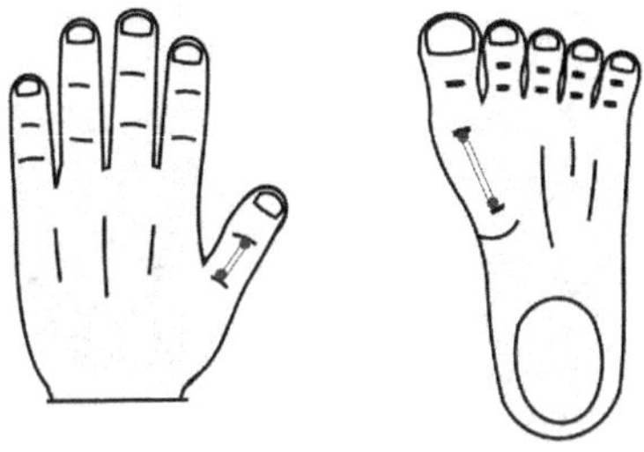

Fig. 76

III. Seed Therapy Through Three Points

In this method, two additional points are taken, alongwith the concerned point. The additional points can be taken in a horizontal or a vertical line.

If additional points are taken vertically, it is called the Vertical Method of Treatment, and If additional points are taken horizontally, it is called the Horizontal Method of Treatment,

For example, let us take the uterus problem. In the Fig. 77 shown below, the Uterus and two more points on the body are shown as dark circles. And then the Uterus correspondence point and two additional points taken horizontally have been taken. Use of seeds on three points is the Horizontal Method of Treatment through 3-point System.

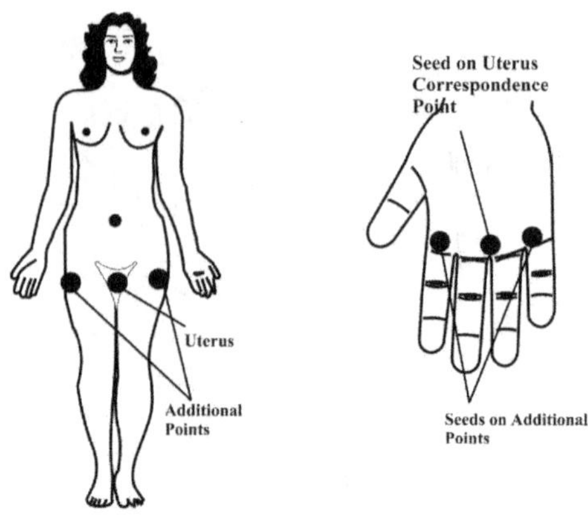

Uterus Problem : Horizontal System
3 Point Method : Seeds

Fig. 77

Let us take another example of problem in lower spine (Fig. 78). It has been shown as a dark circle and two additional points have been taken vertically, also marked with dark circles. Use of seeds on these three points is the Vertical Method of Treatment through 3-Point System.

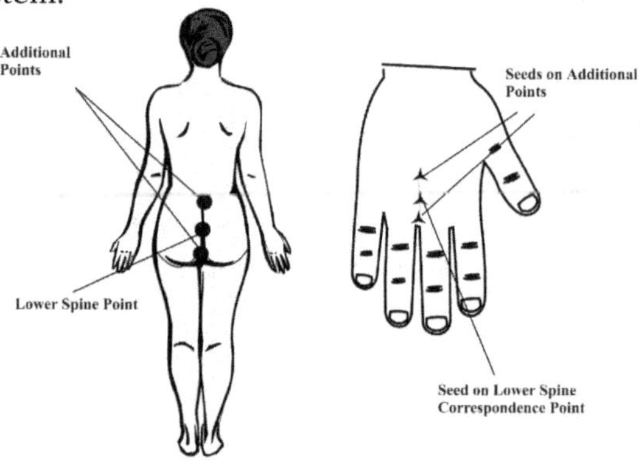

Lower Spine Problem :
Vertical Method : 3 Points

Fig. 78

This method is very convenient method, which esults in prompt cure of diseases affecting any one part of the body.

IV. Five Stages Method : This method is used in grave chronic and systematic diseases.

Ist Stage : Direct use of seed on the affected correspondence point (the primary or secondary correspondence point, where there is a stronger pain reaction).

2nd Stage : Use of seed on additional points. Find out the additional painful points in the area surrounding the painful point. They are called additional points of correspondence. To some extent, the 2nd Method of Horizontal or Vertical Treatment of Points.

Sometimes among these additional points a very effective tender point is located, which gives immediate relief on use of seed. Then, this is considered as the Controlling Point.

3rd Stage : We should know the various organs involved in a particular disease. For example, if there is pain in the liver, we should know which other organs are associated with the liver. E.g. the stomach, small intestine, large intestine, etc. Hence, search these additional points of the other organs involved in a particular disease and use seeds on them.

4th Stage: Then comes the correspondence point in the Spinal Cord. As we know, Spinal Cord has connections with all the organs through various nerves in the body. So search for the painful points in the Spine Correspondence part and use seeds on them.

For ease of reference, I am giving below info which tells you which ailments and organs are connected with which spinal vertebrae.

Ailments and organs connected with spinal cord nerves:

Cervical Vertebrae (C1 to C7) •

C1 **Connected with** : Blood supply to the head, the pituitary gland, and the scalp, bones of the face, the brain itself, inner and middle ear, the sympathetic nervous system
Ailments : Headaches, nervousness, insomnia, head colds, High BP, migraine headaches, mental conditions, nervous breakdowns, amnesia, epilepsy, chronic tiredness, dizziness

C2 **Connected with** : Eyes, optic nerve, auditory nerve, sinuses, mastoid bones, tongue and forehead
Ailments : Sinus trouble, allergies, crossed eyes, deafness, eye trouble, earache, blindness, fainting spell

C3 **Connected with** : Cheeks, outer ear, face bones, teeth, tri-facial nerve
Ailments : Acne or pimples, eczema, neuritis, neuralgia

C4 **Connected with** : Nose, lips, mouth, eustachian tube and mucous membranes
Ailments : Adenoids, all allergies (hay fever), rose fever, catarrh, hard of hearing,

C5 **Connected with** : Vocal cords, neck glands, pharynx
Ailments : Hoarseness, laryngitis, sore throat

C6 **Connected with** : Neck muscles, shoulders, tonsils
Ailments : Stiff neck, tonsilitis, croup, pain in upper arm, whooping cough

C7 Connected with : Thyroid gland, bursa in the shoulders, the elbows
Ailments : Bursitis, goiter, colds, thyroid conditions, tennis elbow

Thoracic Vertebrae (T1-T12)

T1 Connected with : Arms from the elbows down, including hands, wrists and fingers, also the esophagus and trachea
Ailments : Cough, asthma, difficult breathing, pain in lower arms and hands, symptoms similar to carpal tunnel syndrome

T2 Connected with : Heart including its valves and covering, also coronary arteries
Ailments : Heart problems, chest pain

T3 Connected with : Lungs, bronchial tubes, pleura, chest/breast, nipples
Ailments : Bronchitis, Pleurisy, pneumonia, congestion, influenza,

T4 Connected with : Gall bladder and common bile duct
Ailments : Gall Bladder problems, jaundice, shingles

T5 Connected with : Liver, solar plexus and blood
Ailments : Liver problems, anaemia, arthritis, low BP, poor circulation, fevers

T6 Connected with : Stomach
Ailments : Stomach problems, indigestion, dyspepsia, heartburn, nervous stomach,

T7 Connected with : Pancreas, Islands of Longerhans, and duodenum
Ailments : Ulcers, gastritis, diabetes, hypoglycemia

T8 Connected with : Spleen and diaphragm
Ailments : Stomach problems, hiccup, lowered resistence, acute and chronic infections

T9 Connected with : Adrenals or supra-renals
Ailments : Allergies, hypertension, anaemia, hypoglycemia, obesity, and hair loss

T10 Connected with : Kidneys
Ailments : Hardening of arteries, kidney trouble, chronic tiredness, nephritis

T11 Connected with : Kidneys and ureter
Ailments : Acne, boils, pimples, eczema, auto-intoxication,

T12 Connected with : Small Intestines, fallopian tubes, lymph circulation
Ailments : Gas in bowl, sterility, rheumatism

Lumber Vertebrae

L1 Connected with : Large Intestines or colon, inguinal rings
Ailments : Colitis, constipation, diarrhoea, hernia, dysentery

L2 Connected with : Appendix, abdomen, upper leg
Ailments : Abdomen cramps, acidity, appendicitis, varicose veins

L3 Connected with : Sex organs, ovaries or testicles, uterus, bladder, knee
Ailments : Diseases of sex organs, bladder problems, knee pain, menstrual troubles, miscarriages, bed wetting, impotency, change of life symptoms,

L4 Connected with : Prostate Gland, muscles of the lower back, sciatic nerve

Ailments : Sciatica, lumbago; difficult, painful or frequent urination; backaches,

L5 Connected with : Lower legs, ankle, feet, toes, arches

Ailments : Swollen ankles, poor circulation, coldness of legs and feet, weakness in legs, leg cramps, weak arches

Sacral and Coccygeal Vertebrae

S* Connected with : Hip bones, buttocks (Consists of 5 bones fused into 1)

Ailments : Spinal curvature, sacro-illiac problems (Consists of 4 bones fused into 1)

C Connected with** : Rectum and anus

Ailments : Hemorrhoids, piles, pruritus or itching, pain at end of spine on sitting

5th Stage: Then follows the Brain correspondence point, because the Brain has the ultimate control over the entire body. Therefore it is important to tell Brain what treatment we wish to give. So use the same seed on the Brain correspondence point.

Example : Liver problem

Fig. 79 shows the Five Stage Treatment Method for Liver problems :

Ist Stage: Liver - One Point

2nd Stage: Additional Points (Horizontally) - Two Points

3rd Stage: Additional Points for other organs (Three Points : Appendix, LI, Stomach)

4th Stage: Spinal Correspondence Point (One Point)

5th Stage: Brain Correspondence Point (One Point)

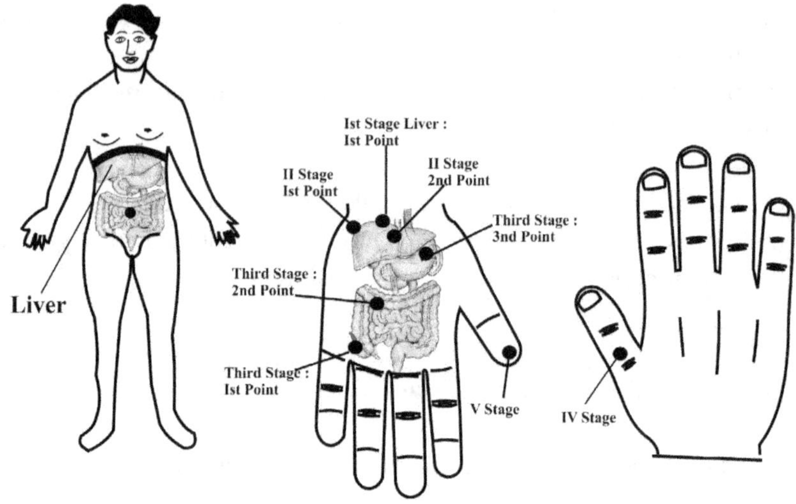

Fig. 79

Use of seeds on Energy Points

There are special energy (basic) points on hands and feet In contrast to the correspondence points of an organ or parts of the body, these energy points have ability to exert strong harmonising influence on the whole organism. Their usage is effective in treatment of acute viral diseases (influenza, cold), chronic diseases, in the period of rehabilitation after operations, in severe injuries, in feeble patients, in spring and autumn for increasing immunity, in elderly people and children, etc.

It is possible to stimulate these points with warm seeds of burning pepper, attached with an adhesive plaster. They are left there till feeling warmth and skin blushing in the place of application. Seeds of various plants are also used.

These Energy Points are available on both sides of hand/foot, i.e. Yin and Yang. In acute diseases use seeds on Energy Points on Yang surface, while in treating chronic, use seeds on Energy Points on Yin surface.

In the diseases of part above the diaphragm, you should treat those Energy Points which are above the diaphragm line on the hand/foot, while in the diseases of the parts below the diaphragm, you should treat those Energy Points which are below the diaphragm line on the hand/foot.

Location of Energy Points on Hand (Fig. 80)

On Yin side

Point 1 : is on the skin crease between the third and fourth fingers.
Point 2 : is at $1/3^{rd}$ of the distance from point 1 on the segment between points 1 and 3.
Point 3 : is located midway between points 1 and 5.
Point 4 : is at $1/3^{rd}$ of the distance from point 5 on the segment between point 3 and 5.
Point 5 : is located at the wrist joint in the middle of the triangle formed by palmar lines.
Point 6 : is located midway between points 5 and 7.
Point 7 : is in the middle of the skin crease at the base of thumb.

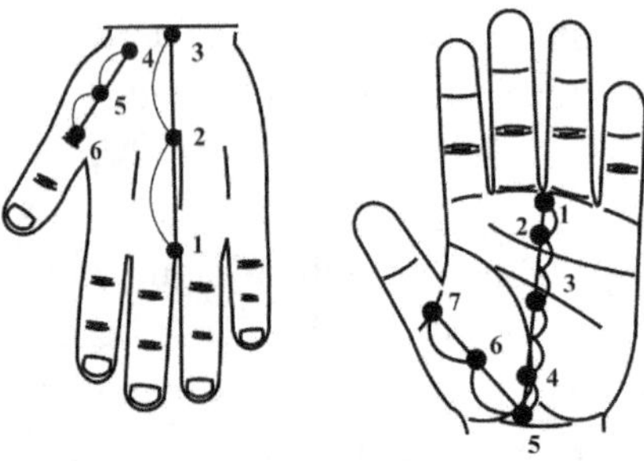

Fig. 80

On Yang side

Point 1 : is on the skin crease between the third and fourth fingers.

Point 2 : is located midway between points 1 and 3.

Point 3 : is at the base of wrist folds.

Point 4 : is in the midddle of the carpometacarpal joint.

Point 5 : is located midway between points 4 and 6.

Point 6 : is located in the middle of the metacarpophalangeal joint of the thumb.

Location of Energy Points on Foot (Fig. 81)

On Yin side

Point 1 : is in the region of the skin crease between the third and fourth toes.

Point 2 : is at $1/3^{rd}$ of the distance from point 1 on the segment between points 1 and 3.

Point 3 : is located midway between points 1 and 5.

Point 4 : is at $1/3^{rd}$ of the distance from point 5 on the segment between point 3 and 5.

Point 5 : is located below the ankle joint line on the Yin surface of the foot (in the heel area)
Point 6 : is located at the base of the first metatarsal bone.
Point 7 : is located midway between points 6 and 8.
Point 8 : is in the middle of the skin fold at the base of big toe

On yang side :

Point 1 : is on the skin fold between the third and fourth toes.
Point 2 : is located midway between points 1 and 3.
Point 3 : is located in the middle of the transversal joint of the tarsus.
Point 4 : is located in the area of the tarsometatarsal joint of the first toe.
Point 5 : is located midway between points 4 and 6.
Point 6 : is located in the middle of the metatarsophalangeal joint of the first toe.

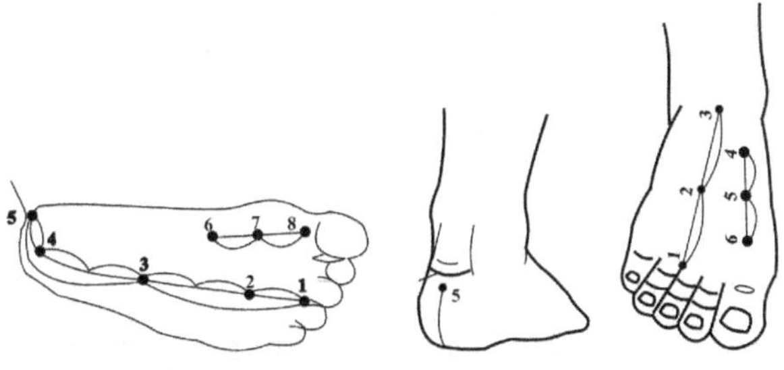

Fig. 81

All energy points can be stimulated simultaneously, or two or three points can be chosen, depending on localization and severity of the patholgical process. For example, in cases of acute diseases it is recommended to use basic points located on the Yang surfaces of the hands and feet, whereas in chronic diseases, basic points on the Yin surfaces. In diseases of organs of the chest the points located above the projection of the diaphragm can only be used (Fig. 82),

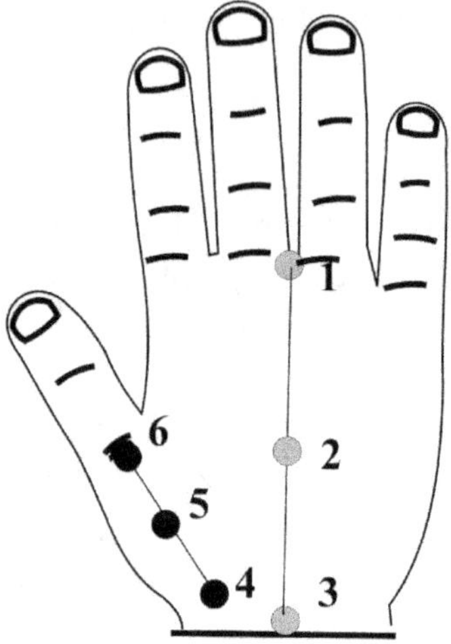

Seeds on energy points (4, 5, 6) above Diaphragm Line for comon cold

Fig. 82

and in diseases of genitalia energy points located in the areas corresponding to the lower part of the abdomen are stimulated (Fig. 83)

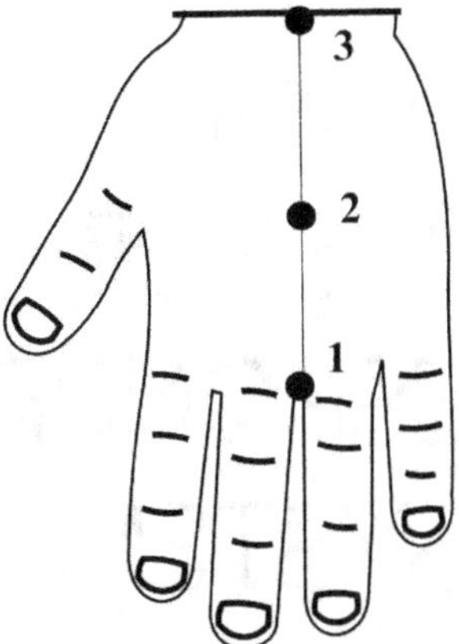

**Use of seeds in genitalia
on the energy points (1. 2. 3)
located below diaphragm**

Fig. 83

The seed therapy through the basic points can be regarded as an independent method of treatment or it can be used in combination with other methods.

CHAPTER SIX

INSECT CORRESPONDENCE SYSTEM

We have studied the Basic / Standard / Original Correspondence System. Now we would study the Insect Correspondence System. As the name implies, it is taken from the way an insect is structured. Following is the figure (Fig. 84) of an insect. It has three portions : head, chest and abdomen plus arms/legs. Similarly, imagine a man sitting in this pose; we can imagine his body in three parts and superimpose it on our finger as shown below (Fig. 85).

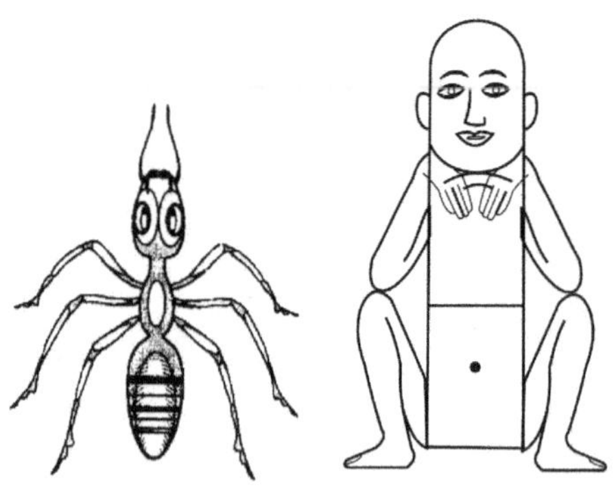

Fig. 84 and 85

Hence, we can easily know as to how to locate the head, chest and the abdomen on a finger/toe. The first phalanx of the finger/toe gives the correspondence points for the head. The second phalanx of the finger/toe would give the correspondence points for the thorax/chest. And the third phalanx of the finger/toe would give the correspondence points for the abdomen. It should be clear that it is on the Yin side of the finger. (Fig. 86)

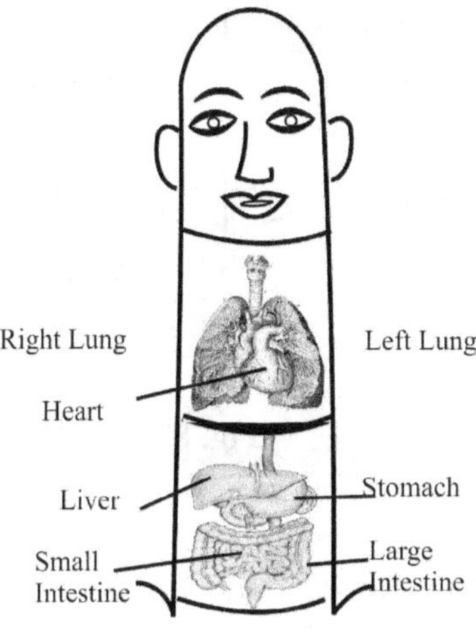

Fig. 86

Similarly, the correspondence points exist on the Yang side of the finger/toe. This side also contains the correspondence points for the entire spine (Fig. 87).

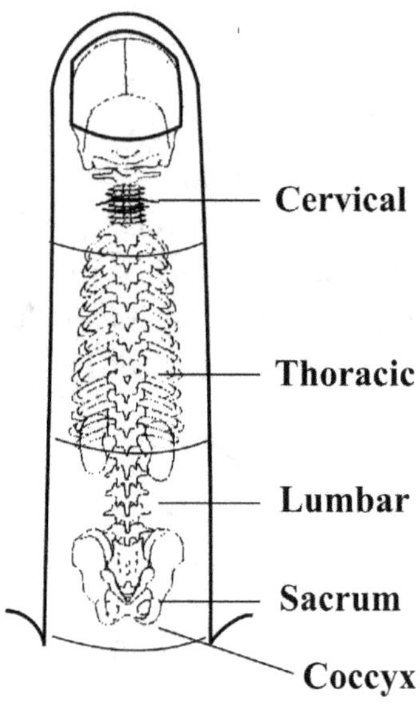

Fig. 87

It also contains the correspondence points of kidneys, ureter, urinary bladder (Fig 88). The left parts will be on the left side and the right parts on the right side of the finger/toe.

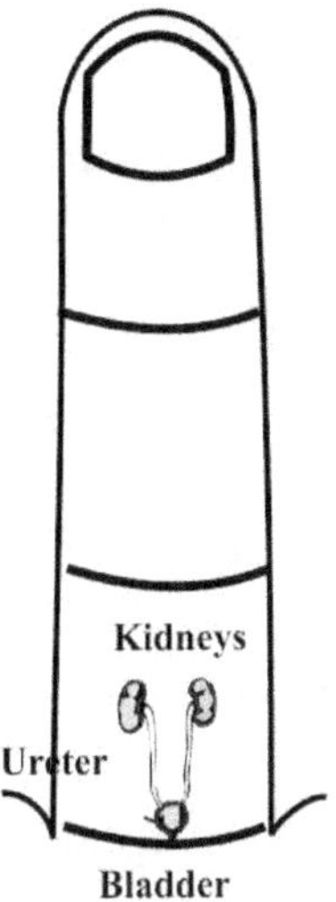

Fig. 88

As shown below, the extremities are flexed in joints. Elbow and knee joints touch each other in the area of the second joint of a finger. Shoulder and wrist joints are projected onto the third joint of this finger, as shown below (Fig.89). The correspondence to the hip and ankle joints are located on both sides of the finger's first joint.

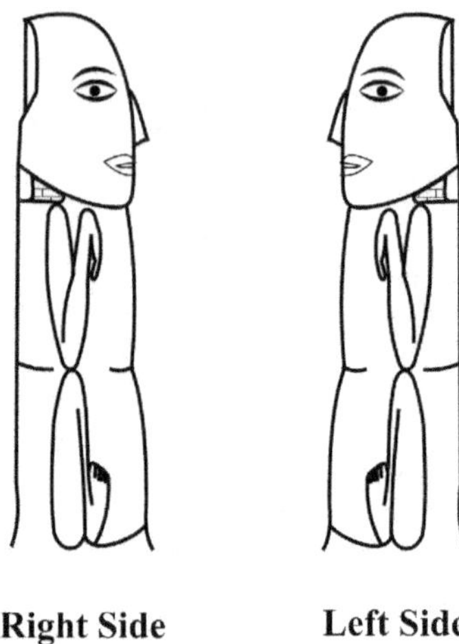

Right Side   **Left Side**

Fig. 89

To locate the Correspondence Points in the Insect System, fingers should be examined in the upward position with their Yin/Yang Surface directed upward, as shown above.

The Yin surface of the body is projected on the Yin surface of the fingers. The Yang surface of the body is projected on the Yang surface of the fingers.

Once the basic position of the insect and the body parts on fingers is understood, it is very easy to understand the various correspondence points on the fingers/toes.

Correspondence Points of a few body organs as per Insect Correspondence System (Figs. 90)

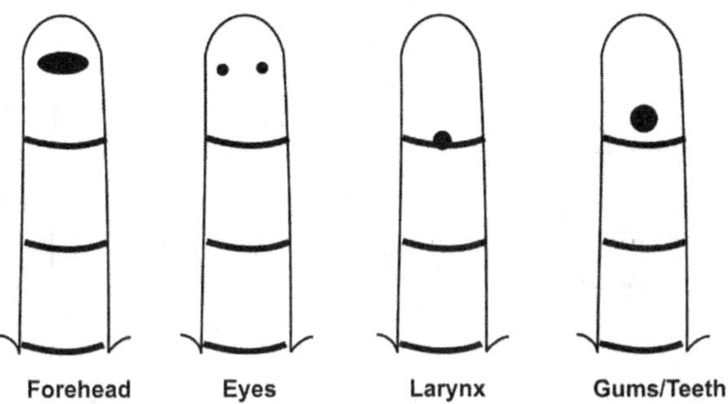

Fig. 90a

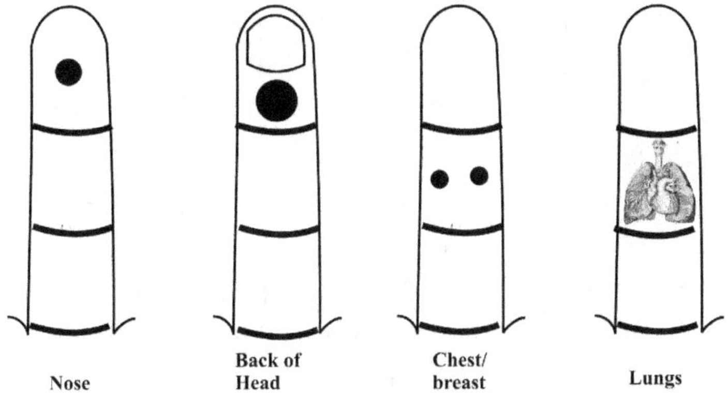

Fig. 90b

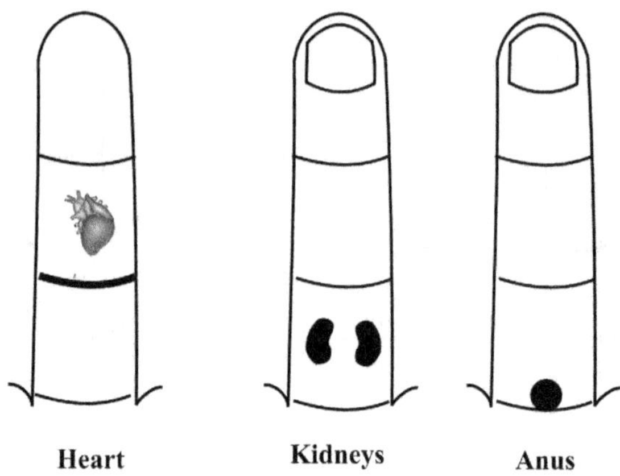

Fig. 90c

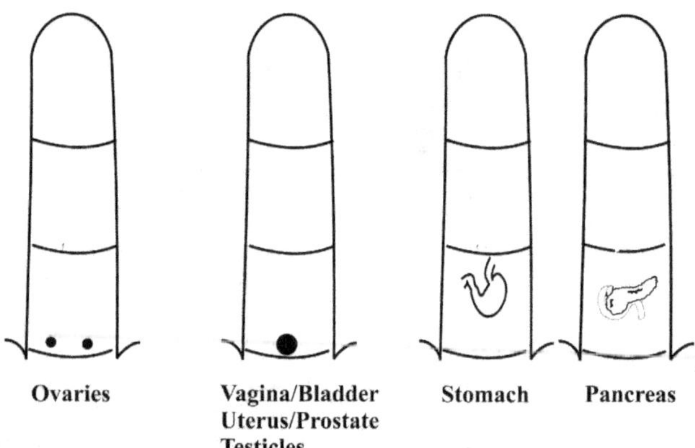

Fig. 90d

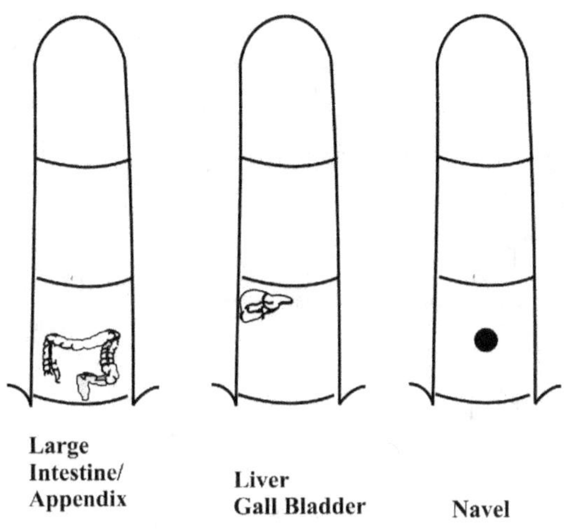

Fig. 90e

Correspondence points for Endocrine Glands (Fig. 91)

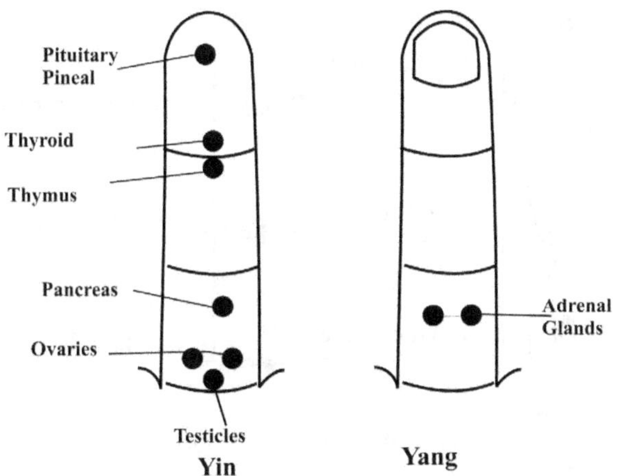

Fig. 91

Joints : Right Side (Fig. 92)

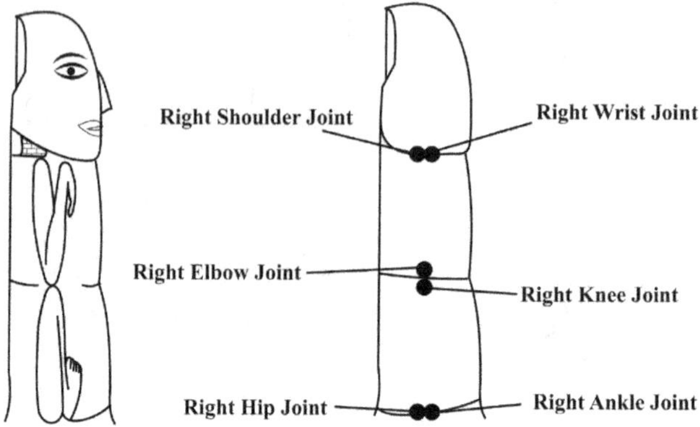

Right side of the Finger

Fig. 92

Joints Left Side (Fig. 93)

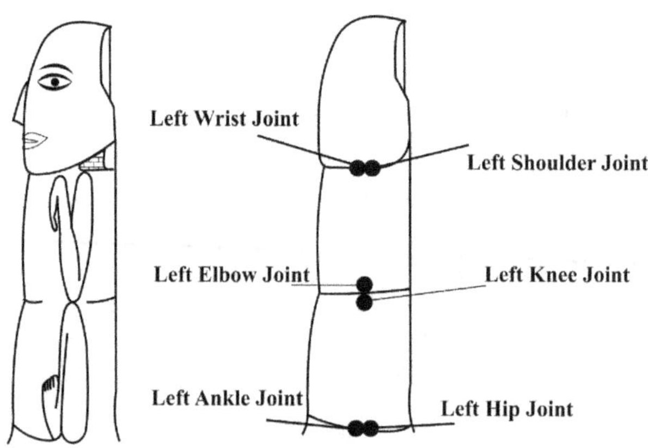

Left side of the Finger

Fig. 93

Energy Points as per Insect Correspondence System (Fig. 94)

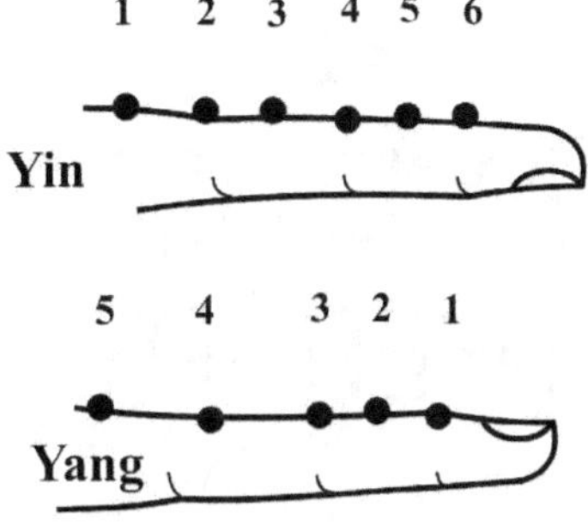

Fig. 94

CHAPTER SEVEN

PRINCIPLES OF SEED THERAPY

In the Seed Therapy, we would learn the use of various parts of plants: leaves, petals, grafts, and especially seeds (fruits).

Interaction of Seeds : As living biological structures, seeds have a great life force necessary for germination and growth of a new plant. During treatment the biological fields of seeds come to interact with the areas corresponding to the affected organs and parts of the body, restoring their energy potential as shown below.

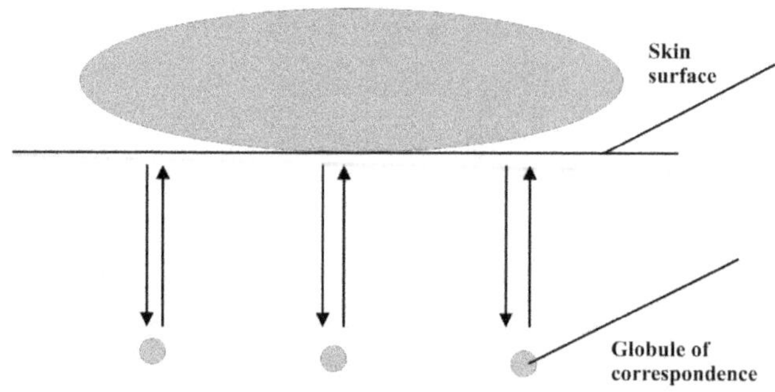

Figure : Action of Seeds

Fig. 95

As a result, seeds can change their structure, shape and colour (become weak, fragile, black, enlarge or decrease in size, crack). All these changes are indicative of active interaction of seeds with points of correspondence, which allows to expect good results of seed application. Following picture shows Interaction of seeds with the globules of correspondence.Fig. 95 as above

The impact of natural materials on a living organism, by the principle of similarity, should be more effective, as the information about the human body is embodied in the systems of correspondence, while seeds (fruits) of plants contain information about the properties of plants.

Seeds and other parts of plants can be applied to the areas corresponding to the affected organs and parts of the body. As a rule, the most painful points are selected. For this purpose all areas corresponding to the lesion is examined with a diagnostic probe or with your fingers.

So find a tender correspondence point on the affected organ as per Standard/Mini/Insect Correspondence System. Affix the seed with the help of an adhesive plaster on the correspondence point. If the seed is correctly put on that correspondence point, on pressing it over, the pain should be felt.

Besides attachment of single seed to the painful correspondence points, the whole area corresponding to the lesion can be covered with seeds. In this case painful «globules of correspondence» need not be searched.

Depending on the area number of seeds applied to the location on an adhesive plaster can vary. If seeds stimulate quite a big area of the skin on the hands and feet (for example, areas corresponding to the Lungs, Heart, Liver, Stomach, Small and Large Intestine), they are stuck arbitrarily on a piece of an adhesive plaster. It is important, that an adhesive plaster with seeds attached to it covers the entire area of correspondence. Picture below shows maize seeds on Stomach correspondence point for chronic gastritis. Fig. 96

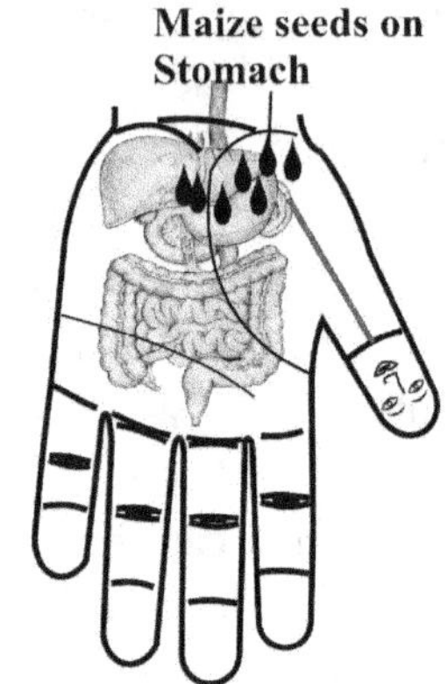

Maize seeds for chronic gastritis

Fig. 96

As regards the area corresponding to the Spinal Column, it is better to attach a strip of an adhesive plaster with a chain of seeds. Following pictures show seeds on the Spinal Column correspondence points as per Standard Correspondence System and Insect Correspondence System for lumbar pain. Fig. 97

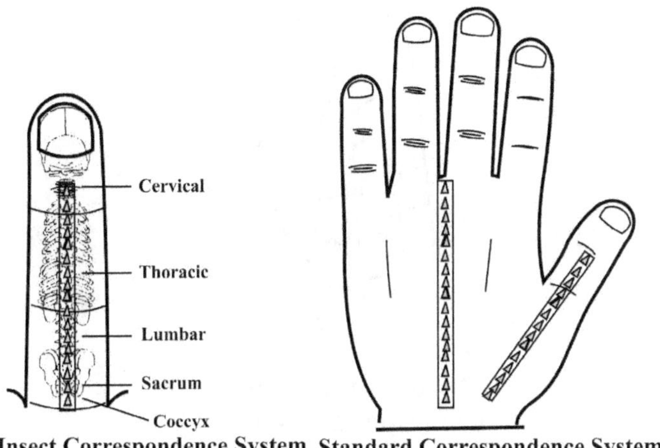

Buckweed Seeds on Spine

Fig. 97

The same principle can be applied for organs, the correspondences of which lie between joints or two adjacent bones (for example, for acting on the areas corresponding to the Rectum, Urinary Bladder, Uterus and Ovaries). The picture in the right margin shows seeds on Uterus correspondence point as per Standard Correspondence System for treatment of menstrual pain. Fig. 98

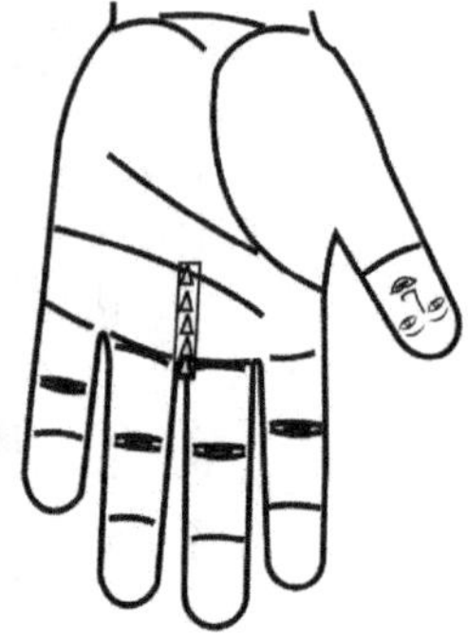

**Seeds on Uterus
Correspondence Point**

Fig. 98

If a correspondence area is small enough (for example, correspondences to the Eyes, Ears, Nose, Teeth, Fingers, etc.), a single seed can be used. The picture below shows application of seed on the Nose correspondence point as per Standard Correspondence System. Fig. 99

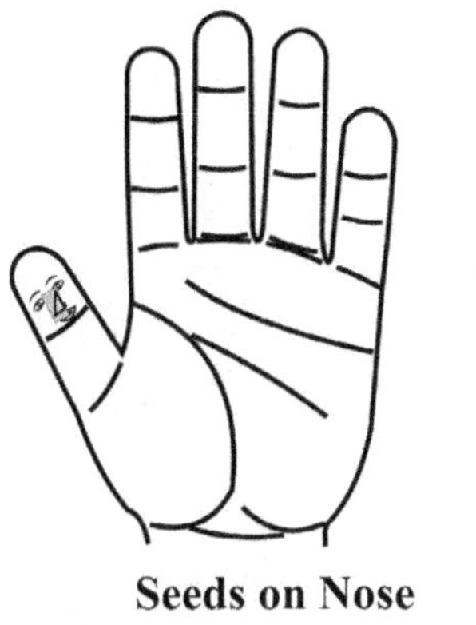

Seeds on Nose
Correspondence Point

Fig. 99

The application of seeds can last from several hours to one day (24 hours). Then, if it is necessary to continue stimulation of the point, they should be replaced by new ones. Often, especially when dealing with children, seeds are applied overnight.

Apart from this, seeds can be used as massagers. For stimulation of larger corresponding areas (correspondences to the Liver, Stomach, Lungs, etc.) hard stones of a peach, a mango, a walnut, a horse chestnut (tree having palmate leaves and large clusters of white to red flowers followed by brown shiny inedible seeds), cones of coniferous trees (of or relating to or part of trees or shrubs bearing cones and evergreen leaves) and ear of corn can be utilised. Following picture shows palm massage by a mango seed. Fig. 100

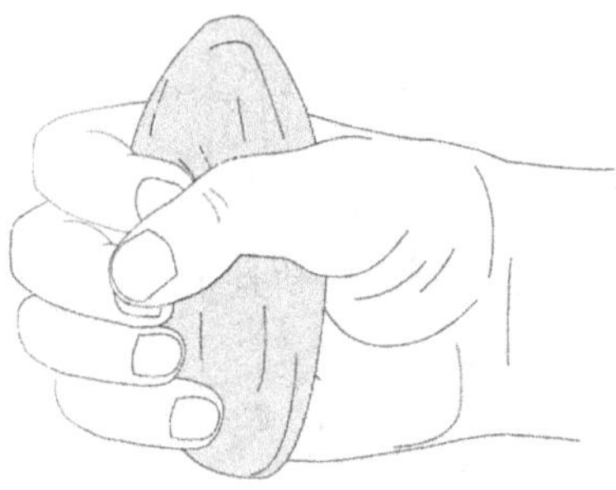

Fig. 100

For medium and smaller areas of correspondence (projections of the Heart, Uterus, Eye, Nose, etc.) it is better to use pips of dates, acorn (fruit of the oak tree), small chestnuts, hazelnut, cones of an alder, ripe ear of wheat, round stones of cherry or seeds of corn, cedar nuts. A piece of a trunk or twigs of a plant, for example, of bamboo, hard stalk of flax can also serve as massagers. Rub a lemon, an onion bulb, potato tuber (a fleshy underground stem or root serving for reproductive and food storage), carrot between hands. Roll peas or nuts with fingers. These are good massagers.

APPLICATION OF SEEDS

A. On the Basis of the Similarity in Shape

Organs and parts of our body are of different shape:
Oblong (Extremities, Intestine, Nose, Lips),
Spherical (Eyes, Head, Breast),
Bean-shaped (Kidneys, Stomach),
Pear-shaped (Uterus, Gall Bladder),
Racemose (Pancreas).

Seeds of similar shape can be used for regulation of morbid processes in internal organs. For example, to help with

Eye Disorders, Head and Mammary Glands - by Round Seeds (Cherry, Black Pepper, Pea);
Cerebropathy(A hypochondriacal condition verging upon insanity, occurring in those whose brains have been unduly taxed): by Walnut;
Heart- by Guelder (Arrowwood, Cranberry Bush), Buckwheat or Pumpkin;
Kidneys, Stomach - by Bean;
Intestines, Veins, Long Bone- by Oats, Brome Grass;
Backbone, Joints - by Bit of Culm (the hollow stem of a grass or cereal plant, especially that bearing the flower) or Carnation Stems.

Following picture shows you similarity between a few plants and body organs :

Similarity of shape of seeds to internal organs (Fig. 101, 102, and 103)

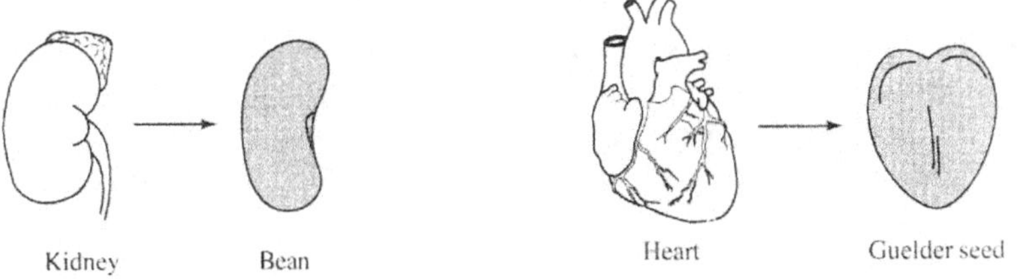

Fig. 101

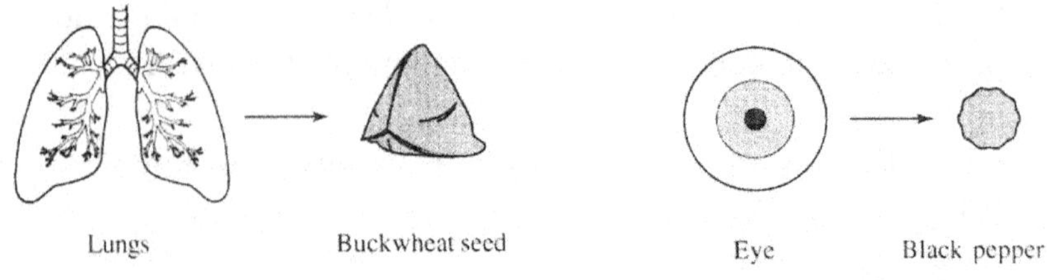

Fig. 102

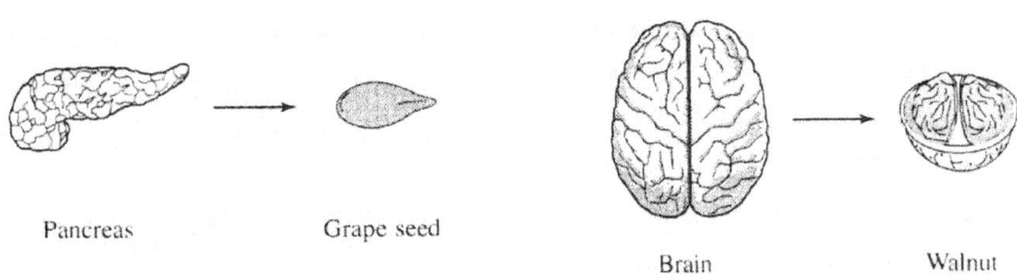

Fig. 103

The stalks of bamboo pinks, cereals and some other plants have articulations resembling joints (as shown below). This means that for getting rid of joints problems the stalks of these plants can be used as massagers or their seeds can be applied to the areas corresponding to the affected joints. Fig. 104

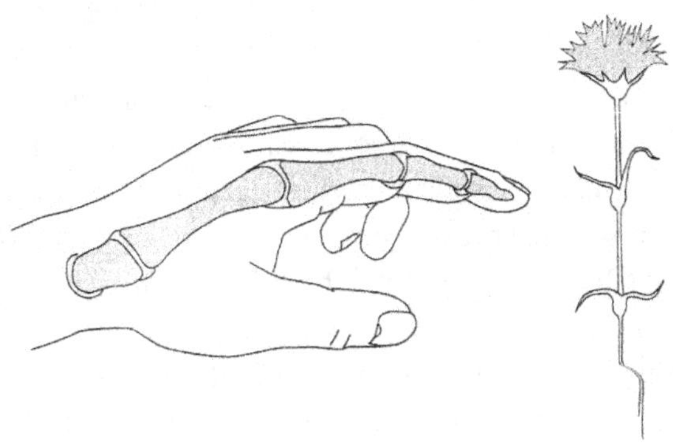

Fig. 104

Similarities between the joints of a pink and the joint of hands

Use of stalks and twigs of plants : There are plants (club-mosses), the stalks of which are similar to the spine, as shown in the following picture, while the structure of the twigs of ferns resembles the thoracic spine with ribs diverging from it. Stalks, leaves and seeds of such plants can be used for improving the affected spine and chest as shown below.Fig. 105

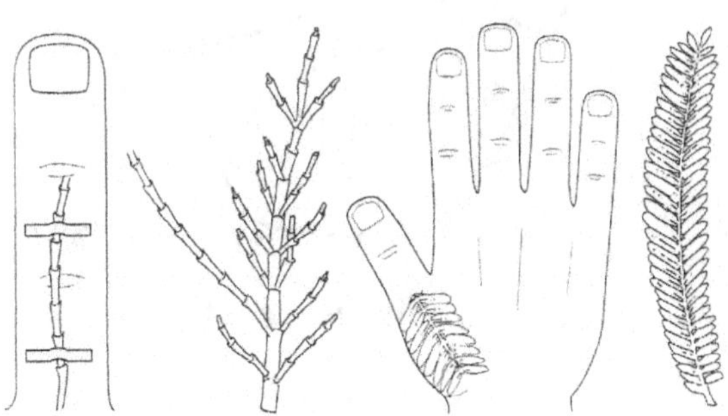

Fig. 105

The berries of mountain ash, guelder, hawthorn grow in clusters, resembling the shape of a thrombus. Seeds of such plants can be applied for diseases associated with increase of blood coagulation, and for prophylaxis (prevention) of thrombosis (the formation or presence of a blood clot within a blood vessel).

Seed therapy for angina pectoris using guelder seeds (resembling heart): In case of angina pectoris guelder seeds can be applied to the areas corresponding to the heart and, in ischemic stroke (deficient supply of blood to a body part (as the Heart or Brain) that is due to obstruction of the inflow of arterial blood (as by the narrowing of arteries by spasm or disease) - to the areas corresponding to the brain, etc. as shown below. Fig. 106

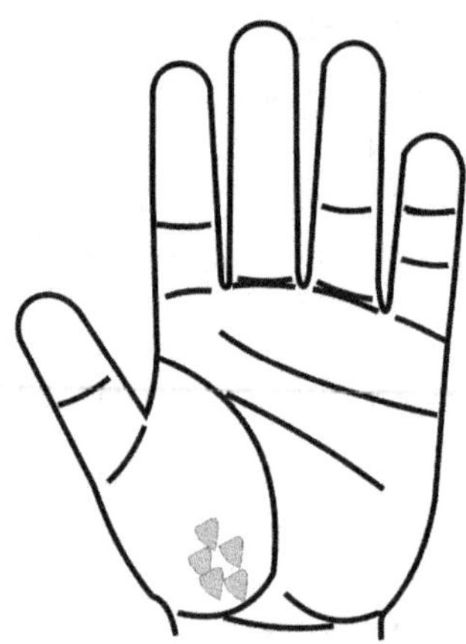

Seeds on Heart

Fig. 106

B. On the basis of properties of plants (Seeds)

If a plant secretes white milk, its seed can be applied to increase the quantity of milk in nursing mothers, and if yellow milk -good remedial effect can be expected while dealing with Liver and Gall Bladder problems.

Some seeds contain a lot of thick juice. They can be used for decreasing inflammatory processes like rhinitis, gastritis, bronchitis, etc. For example, seeds of flax. Seeds of aqueous plants can be applied when there is a pathologic accumulation of body fluids and edema. Picture in the right margin shows Seed in the Lung area for chronic bronchitis using flax seeds as per Insect Correspondence System. Fig. 107

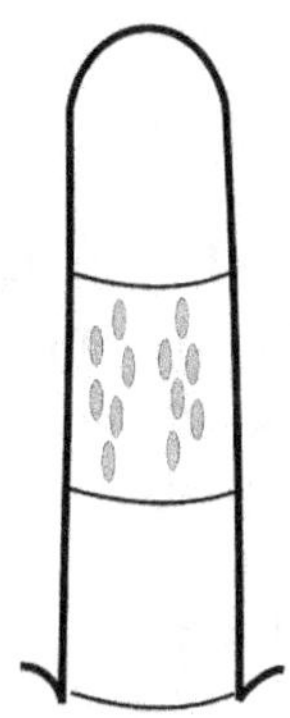

Seeds on Lungs

Fig. 107

The berries of buckthorn, cowberry, cranberry are cold-resistant and do not change their properties on freezing. Their seeds (berries) can be used to relieve a cold, flu.

C. On the Basis of the Mode of Dissemination of Seeds

The mode of dissemination of seeds in nature can also be taken into account for providing health harmonization.

Seeds of many plants are disseminated by air with the help of wind. For this purpose they have «parachutes», like the dandelion, flakes, like the poplar and «feathers», like the maple or ash. There are plants, which spread like tumble-weed. Seeds of such plants are better to apply in cases of joints, ligaments and muscles disorders.

Burdock and bur-marigold have thorns, which cling to clothes of people and wool of animals. Such seeds are better to use for diseases of skin, hair and nails.

Pods with seeds are capable of opening when they grow ripe, then the seeds are disseminated in the surroundings. They can be used for healing of the diseases accompanied with spasms (for example, renal colic, painful menstruation).

D. On the Basis of Rest and Activity Periods of Seeds

The majority of seeds have a rest period. It is a period of time, when the seeds have not germinated yet. They also have a period of activity, when they sprout and give rise to new plants.

According to this, chronic diseases can be better treated by seeds, lying in a state of rest, and acute ones - by seeds in a state of activity (i.e. germinating).

To prolong a period of rest, seeds can be placed in a refrigerator or irradiated with blue, green or violet light, using a device for colour therapy.

To make seeds more active, they should be exposed to orange or red light or simply bright solar light for an hour. Aeration can be carried out by putting the seeds in a glass of warm water and by passing air through the water for two hours with the help of an aquarium compressor. For the same purpose, seeds can be soaked in warm water (25-30°C) and the water should be changed daily till foam appears on the seeds. Seeds covered by hard shells (stone fruits) can be dipped in boiled water for 15 minutes.

E. Use of Information about Medicinal Properties of Plants

Since seeds contain information about the entire plant, one should use knowledge about its medicinal properties.

For example, application of water melon, melon and parsley seeds to the areas corresponding to the Kidneys, increases the diuretic and anti-inflammatory effects. The application of hawthorn seeds to the areas corresponding to the Brain produces a sedating effect, and to the areas of the Heart, helps get rid of functional cardiac disorders and mild forms of arrhythmia (an abnormal rate of muscle contractions in the heart).

Stimulation of the areas corresponding to the brain by the application of Chinese lemon seeds increases working capacity, decreases mental and physical fatigue. When placed on the areas of the medulla oblongata, they boost the activity of the cardiovascular and respiratory centres, as shown in the figure below. Fig. 108

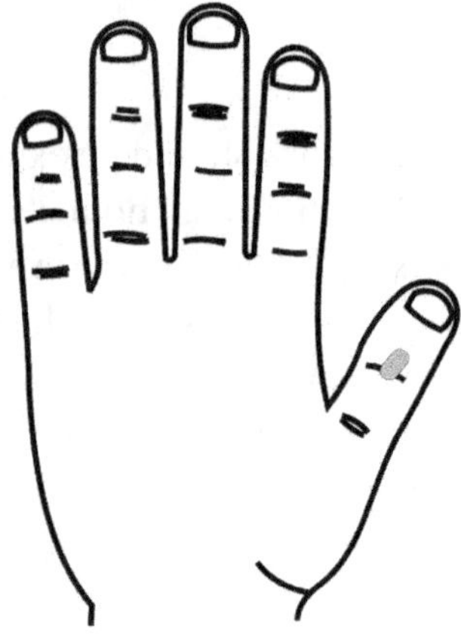

Fig. 108

Stimulation of the points corresponding to the Heart with the seeds of May: Lily-of-the-valley will help in mild forms of chronic heart failure. Seeds of the bird cherry and blueberries having astringent properties can be used in diarrhea, by placing them on the areas corresponding to the Small and Large Intestines. Fruits of fennel and cumin are utilised for their air evacuating and spasmolytic properties in meteorism (distention of the abdomen with gas). Picture below shows use of fennel seeds in the abdomen area in meteorism (gaseous distension of the stomach or intestine). Fig. 109

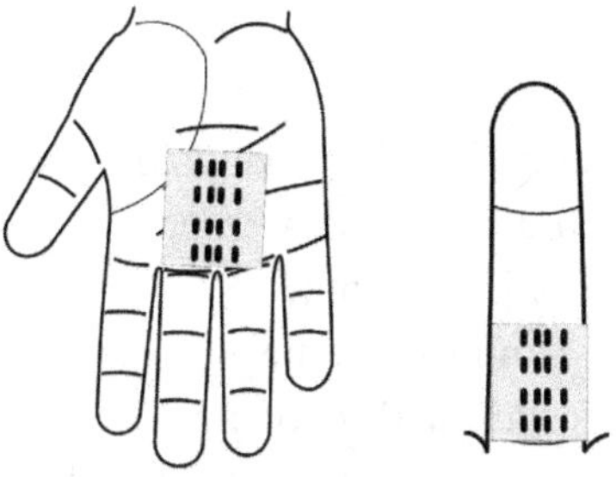

Fig. 109

Horse-chestnut is used for massage of the areas corresponding to varicose veins. The massage should be given from the periphery to the centre.

Wild rose seeds are applied to the area corresponding to the breastbone in diseases of the blood accompanied with bleeding, as shown in the following picture as per Standard and Insect Correspondence Systems. Fig. 110

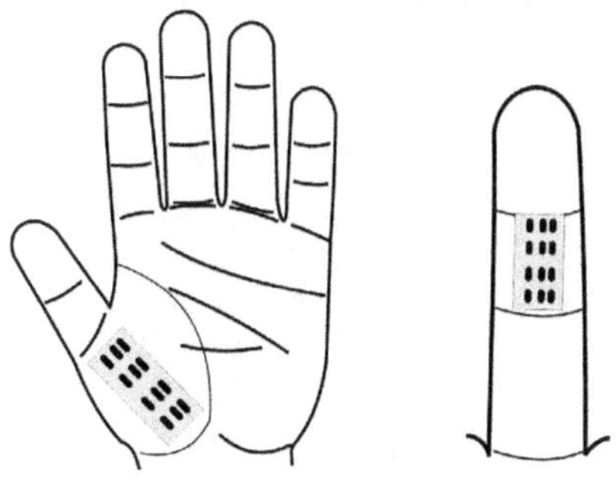

Fig. 110

Seeds of

Pomegranate are used in hearing and vision disorders,
Rice - in bronchitis and bronchial asthma,
Barley - in haemorrhoids and gout,
Flax - in constipation and toothache,
Marigold - in the inflammation of an eye and thrombophlebitis (inflammation of a vein with formation of a thrombus),
Peas - in anaemia and urolithiasis (a condition that is characterized by the formation or presence of calculi in the urinary tract),
Corn seeds - in diabetes mellitus (on the area of pancreas) and epilepsy etc.
Magnolia-vine (on the brain zone) - stimulation of working efficiency, elimination of drowse;
Bird cherry (zones of large and small intestines)- diarrhea;
Briar (dogrose) (zones of liver and gall bladder)- affections of the liver;
Arrowwood (snowball), hawthorn (zones of head and heart)- hypertension;
Dill and Fennel (zones of large and small intestines)-meteorism;
Watermelon (zones of kidneys and urinary tracts) - edema

CHAPTER EIGHT

PRINCIPLES OF SEED THERAPY (Contd)

F. SEEDS AND SIX ENERGIES

Taking into account the shape, colour and taste of seeds, odour of flowers of plants and of their fruits, seeds can be divided into six groups and related to Six Ki, as shown below on the left and Eight-Ki, as shown below Fig 111 and Fig 112 : **Forms of seeds according to Six Ki /Forms of seeds of 2 more Ki as per Eight Ki**

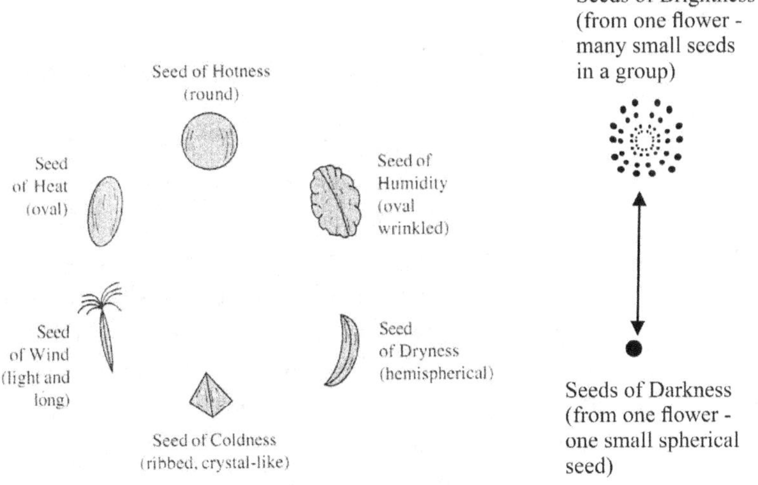

Figs. 111 and 112

i. A group of seeds relating to the category of Wind consists of seeds green in colour, long in shape, and sour in taste. They can be used for improving the work of the Liver, Gall Bladder, Joints, Muscles and Bowel Movement stimulation (for example, in constipation). These seeds can also be used to lessen oedema, obesity and decrease the amount of fluids discharged (rhinitis, lacrimation, diarrhoea, sweating, etc.). Picture below shows use of cumin seeds in constipation, along the LI flow correspondence points. Fig. 113

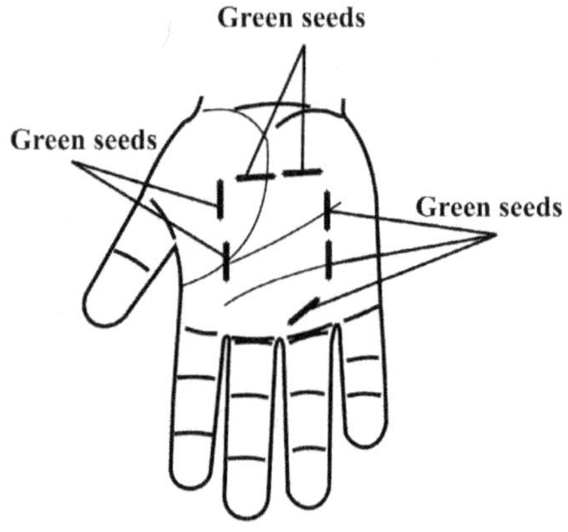

Fig. 113

ii. A group of seeds relating to the category of Heat are applied for normalising the Heart, Small Intestine, blood vessels, and can be also used for getting rid of viral diseases (influenza), cramps and spasms, bronchial asthma, diseases of the blood, better bone fracture consolidation, and other diseases. Seeds red in colour, oval in shape and having spicy taste fall under this category of Heat. Picture below shows the use of red burning pepper seeds for the fractures of the forearm bones in a typical place. Fig. 114

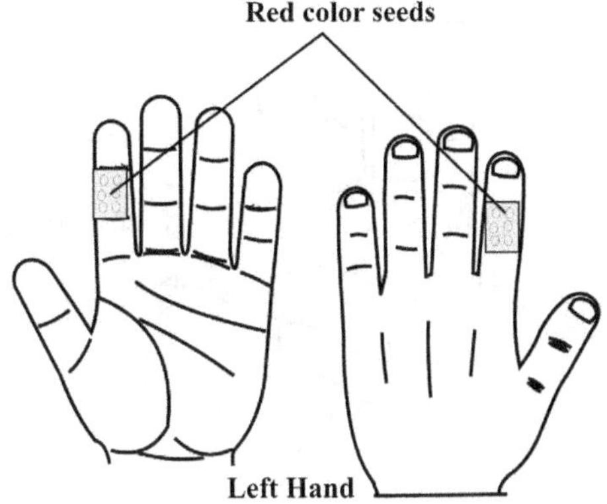

Fig. 114

iii. A group of seeds relating to the category of Hotness is used for general fitness, accelerating the processes of restoration of an organism, and wound healing. They are useful for old people, children and feeble people suffering from chronic diseases. In these cases seeds can be attached to the energy points of hands and feet (You have already studied the Energy points on Yin and Yang of hand/foot). They can also be used for harmonising any organ, especially the nervous system. Seeds orange in colour, round in shape and having pleasant freshening taste come under this group. Picture below shows the use of round pea seeds in general weakening of organism (Yin Energy Points). Fig. 115

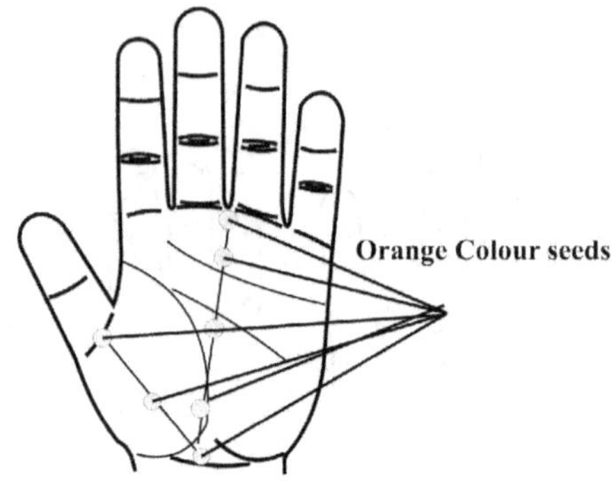

Fig. 115

iv. Seeds yellow in colour, of oval and wrinkled shape and of sweet taste come under the group of Humidity. They are applied for stimulating the activity of the gastrointestinal tract, improving the lymph flow, diseases accompanied by cramps, severe persistent pains, as well as for easing the problems of gallstones and renal stones. Picture below shows the use of yellow corn seeds on Kidney correspondence points for easing out kidney problems. Fig. 116

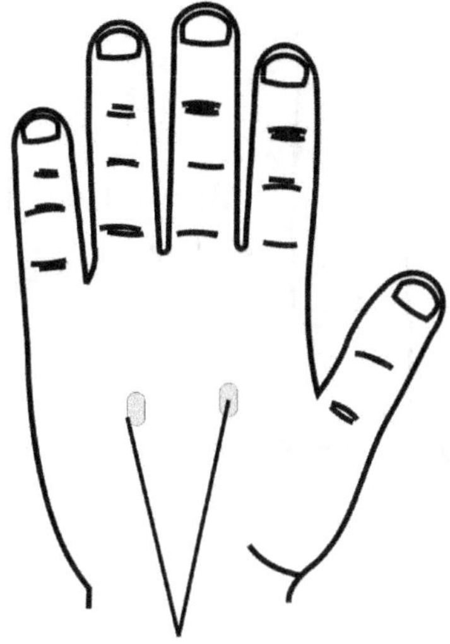

Yellow colour seeds

Fig. 116

v. A group of seeds relating to the category of Dryness is used in cases of the Lungs, Large Intestine, skin and mucous membranes diseases. They are applied in bleeding, rapid heart beat and diarrhea. This group consists of seeds brown in colour, hemispherical in shape and bitter in taste. Picture below shows the use of brown seeds of pear in inflammatory diseases of the lungs. Fig. 117

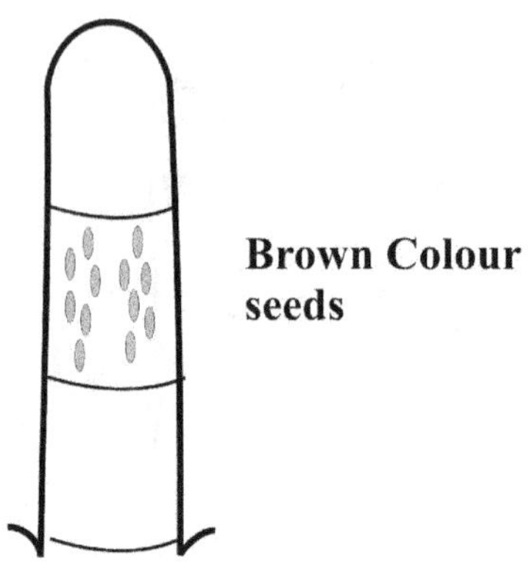

Fig. 117

vi. A group of seeds relating to the category of Coldness is applied in diseases of the Kidneys and Urinary Bladder, for strengthening bones and teeth, and also for fever, oedema, diseases accompanied by the formation of pus, excessive excretion of fluids, and for losing weight. This group contains seeds, black in colour, ribbed (crystal-like) in shape and salty in taste. Picture below shows the use of buckwheat seeds with black shell for cystitis (inflammation of the urinary bladder).Fig. 118

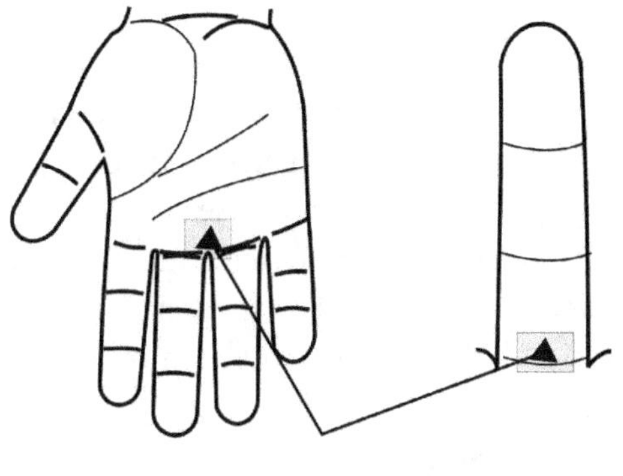

Black colour seeds

Fig. 118

Seed Therapy According to the Direction

The plants, like other living objects, have an energy system which supports their vital activity. In spite of the fact that the circulation of energy is carried out simultaneously in many energy canals, there is a dominating direction of energy flow, which coincides with that of biological growth of plants (as shown below). Fig. 119 : **Predominant direction of energy flow in plants**

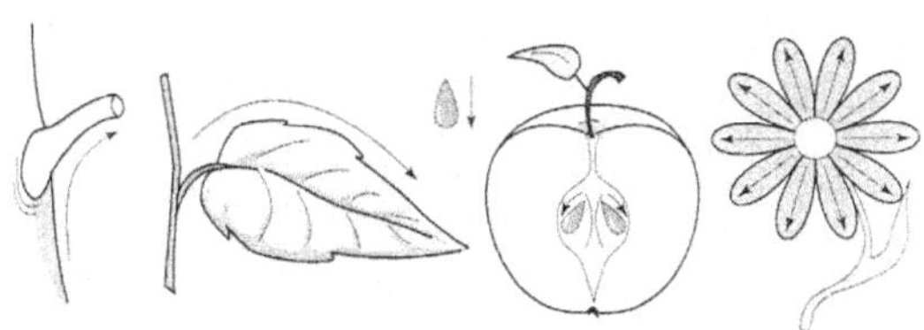

Fig. 119

This property can be used for therapy with seeds and other parts of the living plants in the systems of correspondence.

First of all it is necessary to find in what direction the plant is growing, the one chosen as the instrument of treatment. If we use seeds, we should know the place of attachment of the seed to the mother plant. Sometimes for convenience the place of an attachment of seeds, grafts, twigs to a plant can be marked with the help of a drop of nail-varnish. And then the treatment is given by fixing the seeds with an adhesive plaster in the system of correspondence you have chosen.

Knowing the basic direction of energy flow in this or that part of a plant, it is possible to change (accelerate or inhibit) physiological processes. If the direction of growth of the twig, leaf, seed coincides with the natural direction of flow of food, bile or sputum, their movement is stimulated. If they go in opposite directions, such processes as passing water, stomach and bowel movements are inhibited. For example, for treatment of constipation it is necessary to locate grains in the area corresponding to the colon in such a way that their energy flow coincides with the direction of the bowel movement (as shown below). Fig. 120

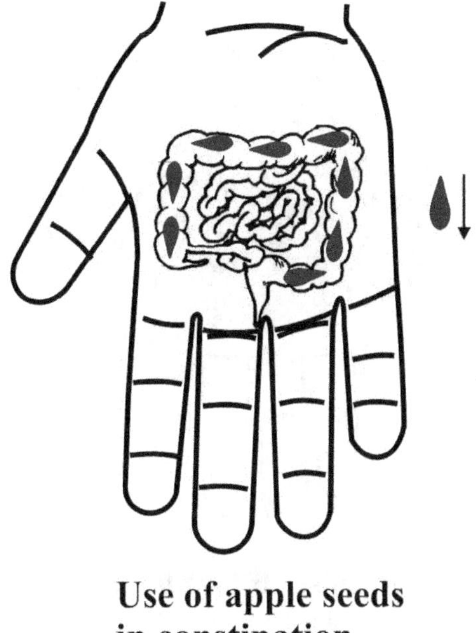

**Use of apple seeds
in constipation**

Fig. 120

Thus intestine will empty faster.

Or the twigs of plants can be placed on the area corresponding to the stomach and oesophagus to slow down their natural peristalsis. It will result in lower appetite.

For obesity problems seeds are attached to the areas corresponding to the mouth and the cardiac part of the stomach (in this case the energy flow of seeds should be in the opposite direction to the movement of food), and also a chain of seeds is applied along the area corresponding to the large intestine, as with constipation, promoting quick evacuation of the bowels (as shown below). Fig. 121

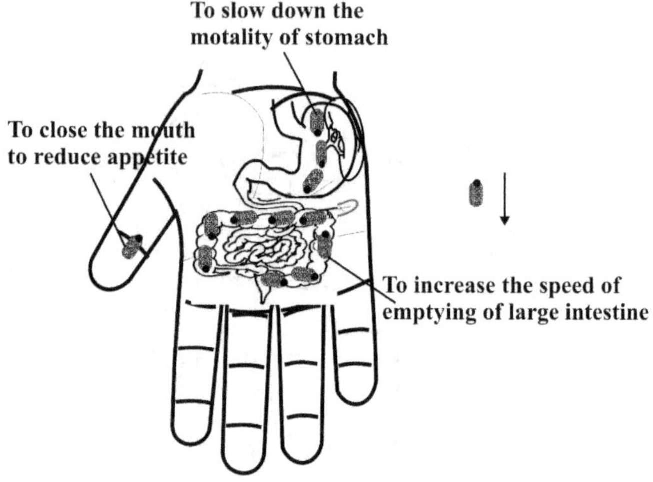

Use of seeds for obesity

Fig. 121

In prolapse of organs, seeds or parts of plants are located in a way as if «supporting» the prolapsing organ (as shown below). Fig. 122

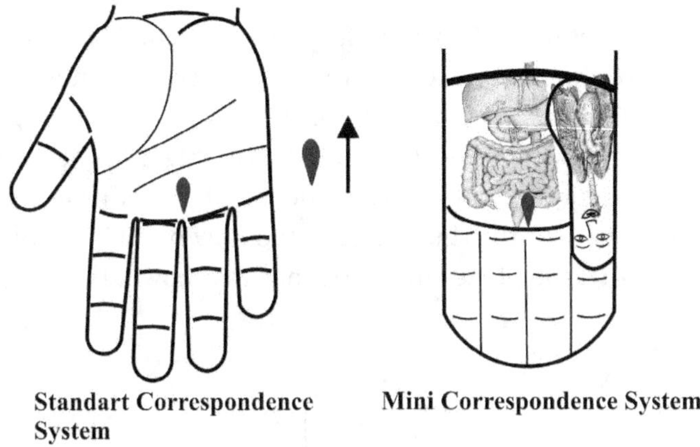

**Standart Correspondence
System**

Mini Correspondence System

Use of seeds for uterine prolapse

Fig. 122

In cases of impotency a twig with a bud diverging from it at an angle can be used (as shown below). Fig. 123

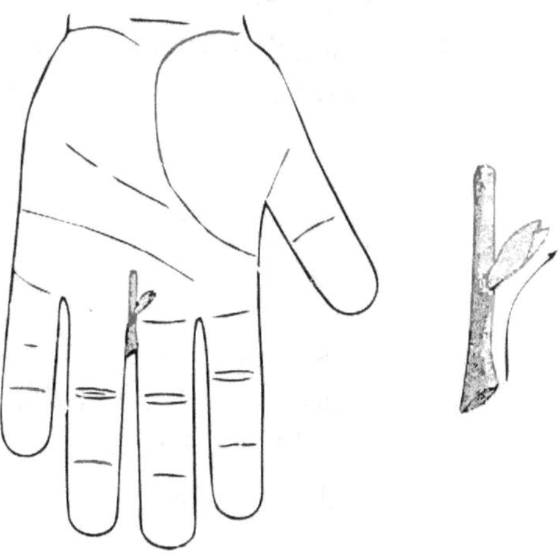

Fig. 123

Some diseases of the Lungs are followed by accumulation of sputum in the bronchi. In these cases we can use seeds as an expectorant. Seeds are located in the area corresponding to the lungs in the direction from the projection of the diaphragm to the trachea (in the standard system of correspondence of hands from the line of life to the base of the thumb). And the flow of their energy should face the correspondence of the trachea (as shown. Fig. 124)

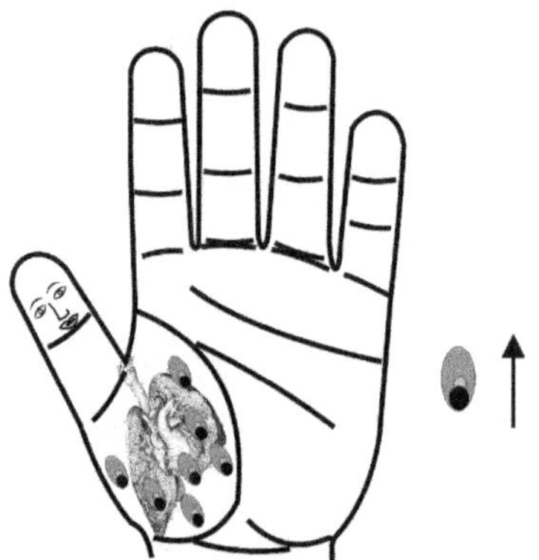

Use of seeds on Lungs for poor sputum discharge

Fig. 124

In some spasmodic processes (for example, renal colic, biliary colic, spasms of peripheral arteries) seeds are applied in such a way that their energy flows are directed from the centre to the periphery, as though dilating the spasmodic zone (as shown below). Fig. 125

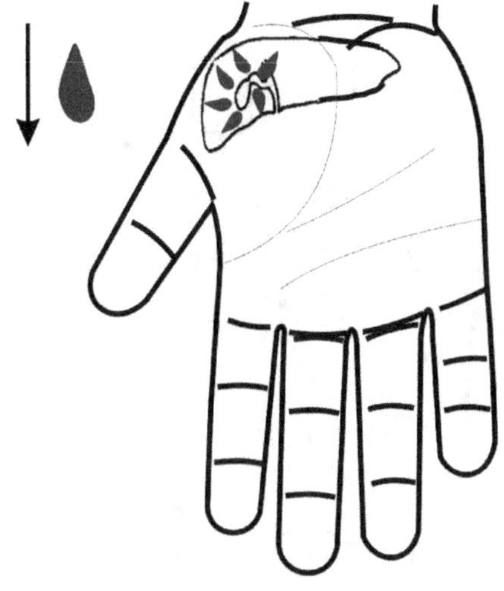

**Use of seeds for
biliary collic**

Fig. 125

Cross-sections of twigs of plants having dilating and resolving action can be used to relieve spasms. Since the stem of plants grows from the core to the bark, naturally, the flow of energy goes from the centre to the periphery.

The necessity to close a hole or exit point of the canal arises in cases of refluxes (back flow of contents of one organ in to another), enuresis (bedwetting) and hernias. In these cases, seeds (needles of the fur-tree, grafts of berries, leaves of plants, the lobes of flowers) are attached in such a way that the flow of their energy be directed from the periphery to the centre (as shown in the right margin).

Fig. 126

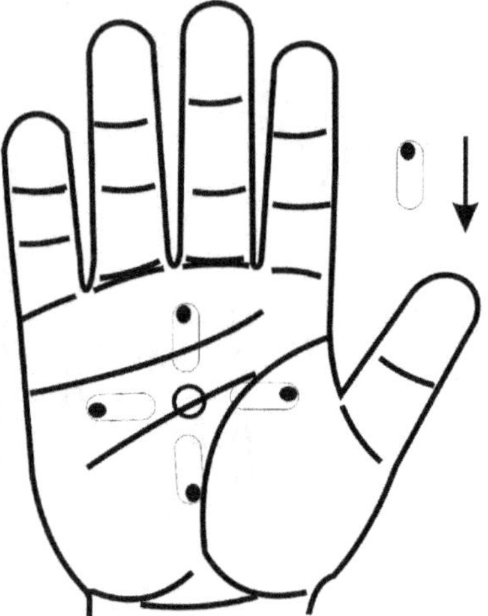

**Use of seeds for
umbilical hernia**

Fig. 126

Rules of Collecting and Storage of Seeds

Seeds and part of plants growing in close vicinity to automobile or rail roads, along the streets in large cities should not be collected as they may contain salts of heavy metals. Preferably, the seeds sold in the shops for planting should not be used, as these seeds may be treated with insecticides or mineral fertilizers. The seeds causing irritation of the skin or belonging to toxicant plants, or causing allergic reactions should not be used.

Do not use unripe, ugly or spoiled seeds (moldy, bad in odour).

Collected seeds should be dried up at room temperature in a well ventilated room, in places which are not exposed directly to the solar rays. After this they should be packed in paper bags and labelled. Stones (pips) after extraction from the fruits should be carefully washed, and dried up. Seeds of citrus fruits cannot be stored and are used just after extraction from the fruits.

In ancient times people who went to gather plants for medicinal purposes fasted for three days, had a wash and put on clean clothes. Before gathering plants they said an expiatory prayer, asking the plant to forgive them for taking a part of it.

People never took more than necessary, never used the young plants so that they did not perish. After the collection of herbs follows thanksgiving. If the entire plant had to be taken, a piece of bread or coin was left in the hole - as ransom. It would be a good thing for us to remember these rules. Let us care about plants, then the results of seed therapy will be better and will not keep us waiting.

Restoring health by using seeds and other parts of plants in systems of correspondence has a number of interesting aspects, which allows to put the method beyond the framework of routine acupuncture and acupressure. The seeds therapy as an effective and safe method of improving health can be recommended for the use not only by medical personnel but also by the lay persons for making relief in simple diseases.

More Examples

1. Varicose vein of the lower limbs : Use of apple seeds

Find out the painful points corresponding to the interior surface of the shin in the Standard Correspondence System on hands, and stimulate them by apple seeds (as shown in the right margin). Fig. 127

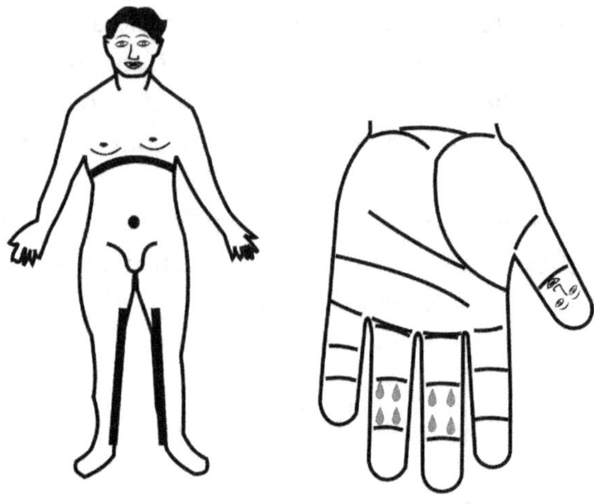

Use of apple seeds for varicose veins

Fig. 127

2. Pains in the frontal and maxillary sinuses region

Apply seeds to the most painful points corresponding to the sinuses of the nose in the Standard Correspondence System of hands (as shown below). Fig. 128

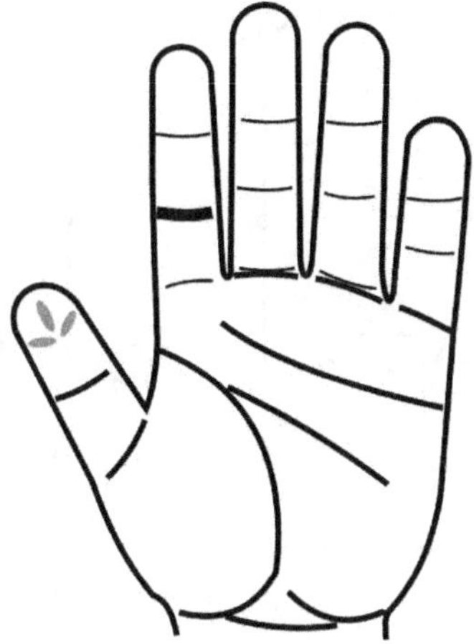

Use of seeds for sinusitis

Fig. 128

3. Chronic otitis : Use of Buckwheat seeds

Apply buckwheat seeds to the areas corresponding to the Ears and Kidneys in the Mini Correspondence System (as shown in the right margin). Fig. 129

Use of seeds for otitis

Fig. 129

4. Post injection abscess Buckwheat seeds

Apply a buckwheat seeds on the point corresponding to the abscess of the left buttock as per Standard Correspondence System (as shown in the left margin). Fig. 130

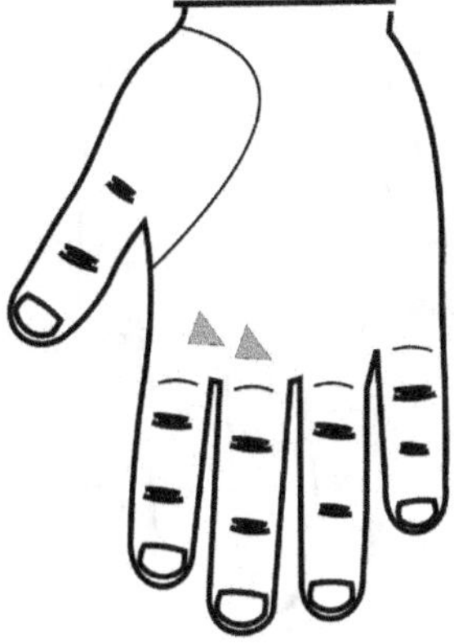

**Use of buckwheat seeds for
abscess of left buttock**

Fig. 130

5. Pains in the left knee joint : Black Pepper corns

Apply black peppercorns) to the correspondence points of the
Knees as per Standard Correspondence System and massage the
fingers by the elastic ring. Fig. 131

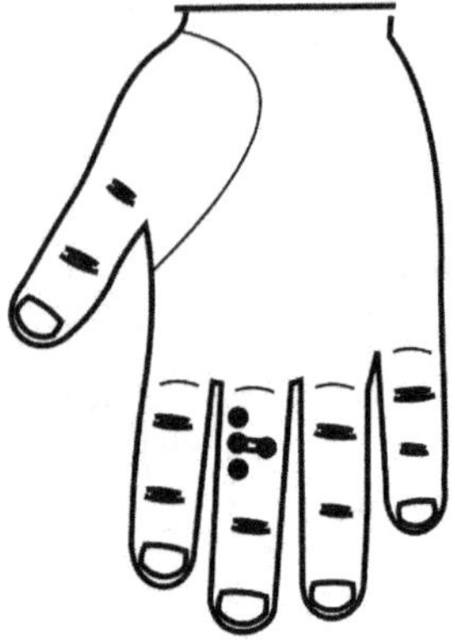

**Use of black pepper for
pain in the left knee joint**

Fig. 131

6. Gout Buckwheat seeds

Apply buckwheat seeds on the correspondence points of the affected parts. Fig 132

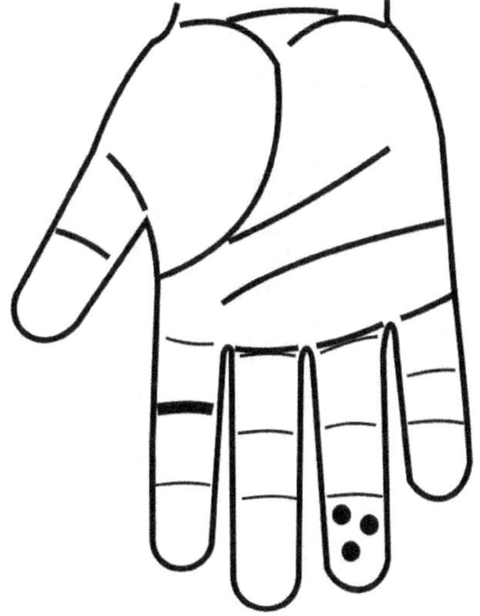

Use of seeds for gout in the finger

Fig. 132

7. Sand in Gall Bladder resulting in heaviness in the right hypochondrium and severe headache in the temporal regions with radiation to the back of the head.

Stimulate the points corresponding to the Liver, Gall Bladder and Temporal region in any correspondence system and apply corn and buckwheat seeds. Fig 133

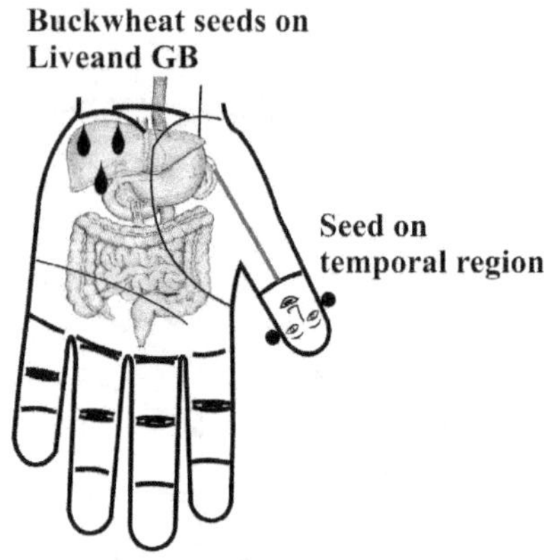

Fig. 133

8. Pain in the lower thoracic spine : Use of Apple grains

Find the painful points corresponding to the spine in the Standard Correspondence System on hands and massage them and apply apple grains overnight (As shown in right margin). Fig. 134

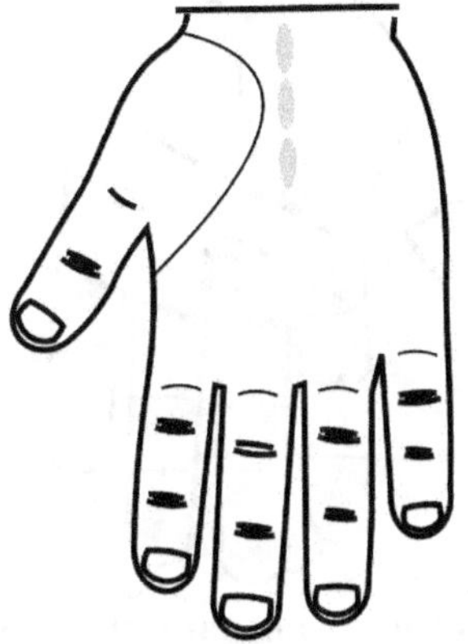

**Use of apple grains for
thoracic pain**

Fig. 134

9. Severe pains during periods

Apply red pepper seeds to the points corresponding to the Uterus on the hand as per Standard Correspondence System (As shown below). Fig. 135

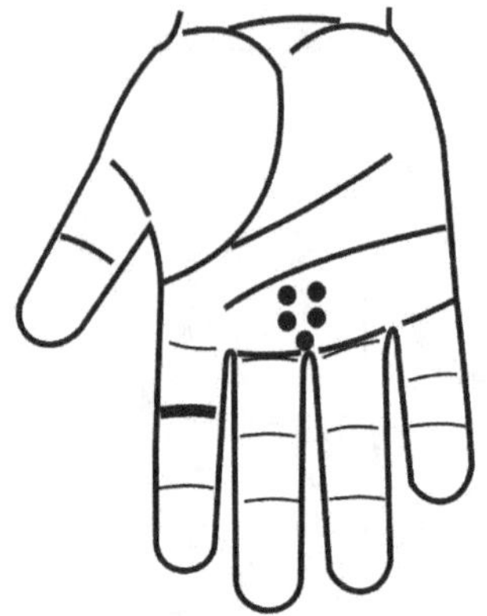

Use of seeds for painful periods

Fig. 135

10. Migraine

Apply buckwheat seeds on the affected corresponding point and also massage the point.
Fig 136

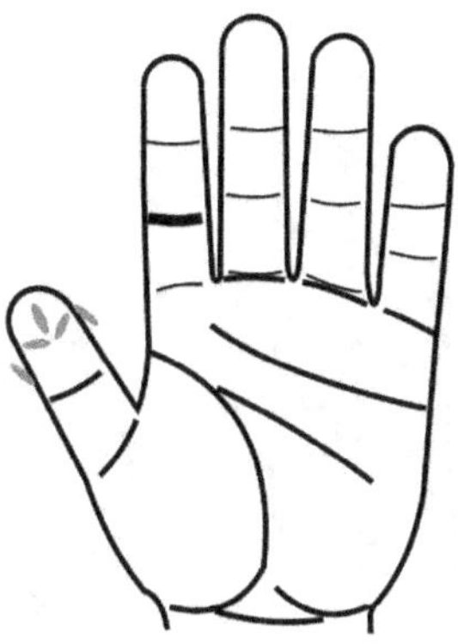

Use of seeds for migraine

Fig. 136

11. Severe pains in the urethral region which increases after urination.

Apply millet seeds to the points of correspondence in hand and foot as per Standard Correspondence System (as shown below). Fig. 137

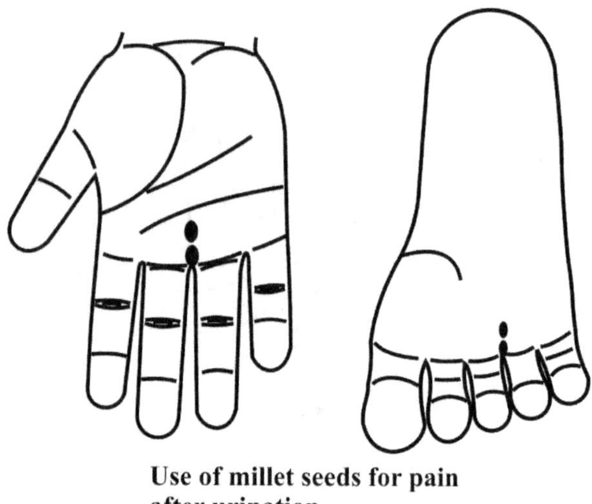

Use of millet seeds for pain after urination

Fig. 137

12. Frequent colds

Apply black pepper corns on the correspondence points of Bronchi and Lungs. Fig. 138

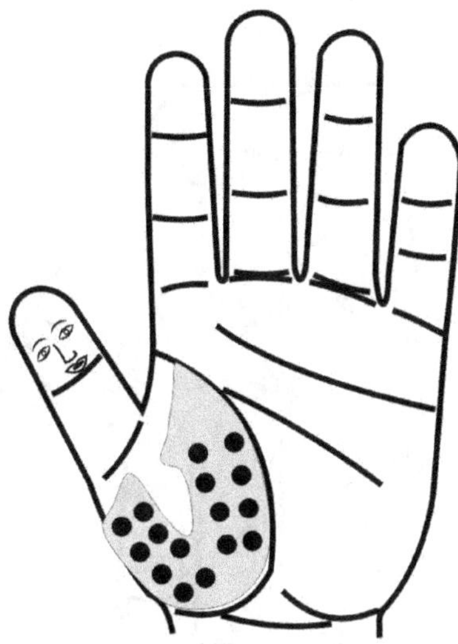

**Use of black pepper corns on
Lungs Correspondence points**

Fig. 138

13. Pains in the right shoulder with limitation in movement of the right shoulder joint on lifting the hand up.

Apply buckwheat grains on the points of correspondence (as shown below). Fig. 139

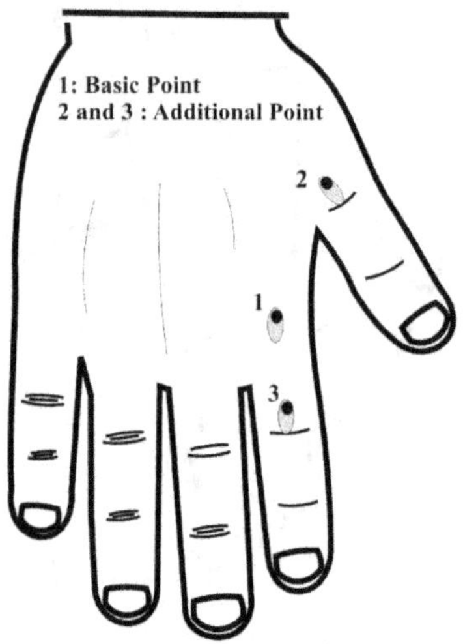

**Use of buckwheat grains
for shoulder pain**

Fig. 139

14. Chronic gastritis with hyposecretion.

Apply pumpkin seeds to the area corresponding to the Stomach in the Insect Correspondence System (as shown in right margin). Fig. 140

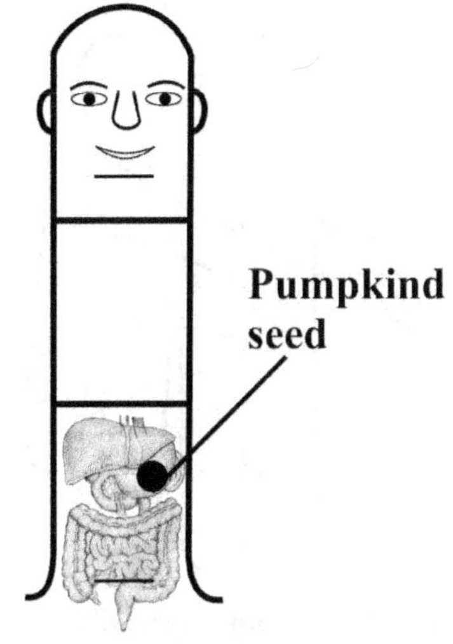

**Use of Pumpkind seed
on Stomach point**

Fig. 140

15. Uterine bleeding

Apply Black pepper corns on the points corresponding to the Uterus in the Standard Correspondence System of Hand. Fig. 141

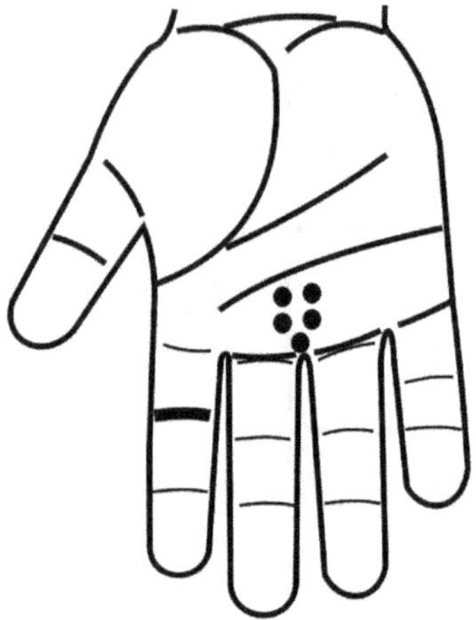

**Use of seeds on uterus point
for uterine bleeding**

Fig. 141

16. High temperature of 39°C and a sore throat

Use lentil seeds on the point corresponding to the Throat in the Insect Correspondence System.

Also, apply black radish seeds on the painful points in the area corresponding to the Head (as shown in right margin). Fig. 142

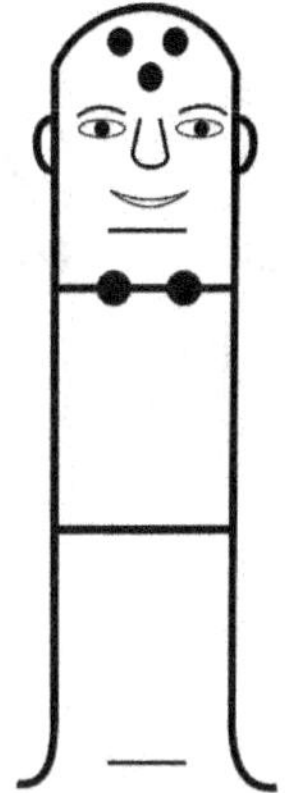

Use of seeds for sore throat and high temperature

Fig. 142

17. Complaints of edema in the left knee joint region after falling.

Apply buckwheat seeds to the painful points of correspondence - left knee.

18. Numbness of the hands at night

Apply lentil grains in the areas corresponding to the wrist joints on both hands and on Yin and Yang sides (as shown below). Fig. 143

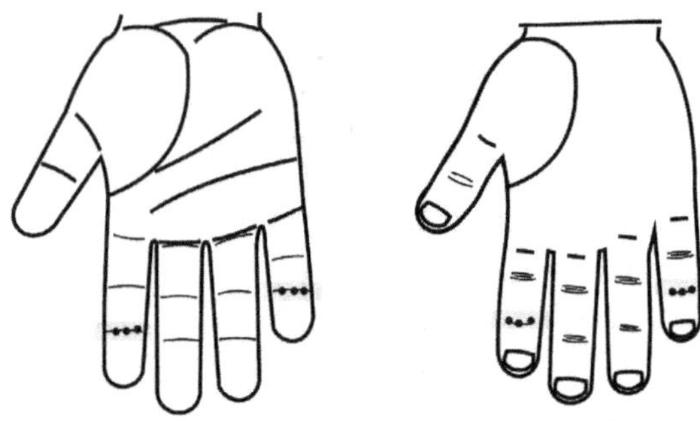

Use of lentil grains on wrist joints

Fig. 143

19. Pains in the lumbar region of the spine in motion and at rest.

Apply Black pepper seeds on the correspondence points of the affected parts in the Standard Correspondence System on hands. For better results use on both hands.

20. Weakness of the sphincter of the urinary bladder, resulting in the incontinence of urine induced by coughing and exercise.

Apply Grape seeds to the area of the urinary bladder in the Standard Correspondence System on hands (as shown in right margin).Fig. 144

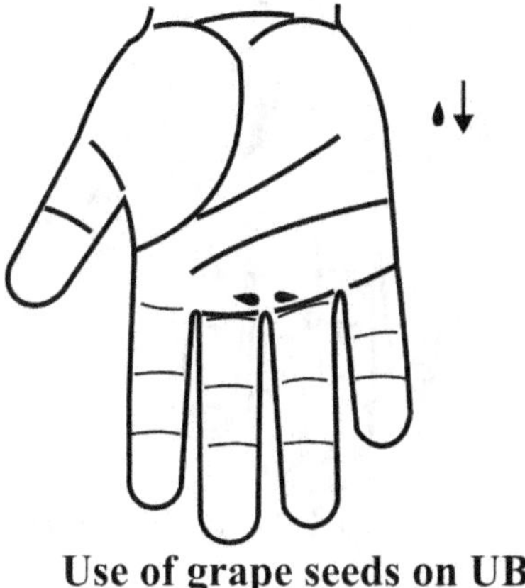

Use of grape seeds on UB

Fig. 144

21. Complaints of hypersensitivity to cold and persistent chilliness.

Apply red beans to the area corresponding to the Kidneys (As shown below). Fig. 145

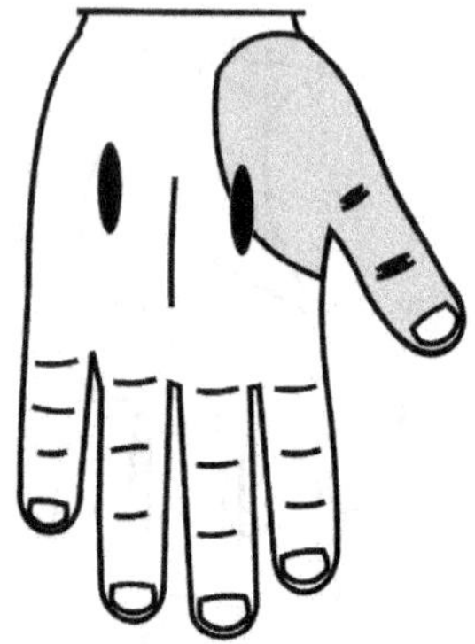

Use of Red Beans on Kidneys

Fig. 145

In short, Seed Therapy can be summed up as under :

Coniferous needles, leaves, petals, grafts and especially seeds (fruits) are powerful and very efficient for stimulation of therapeutic points and correspondence areas on hands and feet.

Plant's seeds are living biological items having mighty energy and own magnet fields.

Such seed can easily come in contact with an energy of a human-being engulfing malignant energy and giving a vital and healthy energy in turn. It is very often the seeds mutate-shrivel, crack and even crumble after treatment. Seed therapy is complete fool-proof, painless and comprehensible plain to everybody.

Furthermore, long-term illnesses are treated by seeds in a quiescent state, acute diseases - by almost sprouted kernels. It is very effective a massage with large seeds or stems of chestnut, walnut, stone of mango, strobile, maize (corn) ear.

Usually seeds or other parts of plants are attached with sticking plaster directly to unhealthy organs or those parts of palms and feet which correspond to them. The most painful points are selected with the help of diagnostic probe, or just toothpick, match, etc. The consecutive pressing on such points should be of equal force. If you are not sure that you can hit plumb centre, attach several seeds so that to cover supposed zone with them.

The application of seeds can last from few hours to one day or several days, if it is necessary to continue stimulation of the point, they should be renewed. Seeds have a great life force and come to interact with affected organs and restores their energy potential. After treatment seeds can change their structure, shape, color (lose energy potential, become fragile, black, enlarge or decrease in size, shrivel, crack or even fall to pieces). But it is not advised to use the plant seeds which are poisonous or allergenic for you or environmentally unsound products, also don't fit green, defective or dead seeds.

Seeds can be used as massagers. To stimulate larger corresponding zones (zones of stomach, liver, lungs) you can use peach, mango stones, walnut, horse chestnut, cones of coniferous trees. For smaller and medium zones of correspondence (heart, urinary bladder, eyes, nose) you can use the stones of dates, acorn, chestnut, hazelnut, alder cones, ripe wheatear, stones of cherry or corn seeds, cedar nut. Bamboo's trunk or twigs, stalk of flax, lemon, onion bulb, potato tuber, carrot can also be used as massagers.

The seeds can be selected due to configuration which resembles the shape of an organ.

Seeds of similar shape can be used for regulation of morbid processes in internal organs.

The seed stores an information about whole plant and possesses its healthfulness. If you know effects of drug plants it will be easier to pick necessary seeds to cure your disease.

Along with the seeds, plants can also be used. For instance, the stalks of bamboo, pinks, cereals and other plants resemble finger, hands, feet joints. To heal joint problems the stalk of these plants can be used as massagers or applied to the corresponding zones of joints.

There are some plants resembling the shape of spine, so, the twigs of fern resemble a thoracic spine. Stalks, leaves and seeds of such plants can be used for spine and chest curing.

Some seeds, for example, seeds of flax contain a thick juice, they can be used for curing of inflammatory processes accompanied by myhopoiesis (rhinitis, gastritis, bronchitis). Similar seeds can be applied if there is a malignant accumulation of body fluids and edema.

Clusters of mountain ash, guelder, hawthorn resemble the shape of a thrombus. Such seeds can be applied for diseases associated with increase of blood coagulation and as a prevention of thrombosis. The berries of buckthorn, cowberry, cranberry are cold-resistant and do not change their properties on freezing. Their seeds (berries) can be used to relieve a cold, flu. In summer, early morning in the country, walk barefoot on the grass till the dew dries up, and feel Nature's force in your hands, feet and your entire body.

CHAPTER NINE

BYOL MERIDIANS

So far you studied Seed Therapy as per different correspondence points on hands and feet. You learnt how to use seeds, which seeds to use and where to use them. Now you will learn Seed Therapy based on Six Ki Theory. Ki means energy and there are Six Ki's on each meridian, imbalance of which causes many disorders. How that imbalance can be restored with the help of seeds is discussed here. But before we go to Six Ki, we have to understand Meridians because these Six Kis exist on each meridian.

A. Energy Flow through Meridians

Chinese Acupuncture

Over 5,000 years ago, the ancient Chinese discovered a subtle energy in the body that can't be seen, felt or found with the senses. Energy disturbances in the subtle bodies precede the manifestation of abnormal patterns of cellular organization and growth.

The Chinese discovered and identified twelve acupuncture meridians along which this energy travels in the human body. Acupuncture meridians are like copper traces on an electronic circuit board, running throughout the body. They were named by the life function associated with them.

Meridians are the pathways of the positive and negative energy power, which carries on some of the communication between the various parts of human beings.

Through these meridians passes an invisible nutritive energy known to the Chinese as Chi or Qi. In India this is known as Vital Force or Prana or Prana Shakti or Jeevani, etc, also known as Ki in Japan.

It may also be understood that each Meridian is on both sides of the body, that is, left and right. For example, Lung meridian is on the left arm as well as on the right arm.

Chi

The word Chi has many translations--nearly every culture in the world has a word to express this concept--but it can be thought of as the activating energy of the universe. Chi is the pure, harmonizing and free-flowing energy that sustains all of life. Chi condenses and disperses in alternating cycles of negative and positive (Yin and Yang) energy, materializing in different ways, forms, and shapes.

It can be neither created nor destroyed. Instead, Chi transforms itself and reappears in new states of existence. All states of existence, therefore, are temporary manifestations of Chi, especially those of physical matter.

Chi is the source of all movement in the universe. The motions of the stars and planets, the radiation from the sun, and the patterns of our thoughts and emotions occur because of Chi. It is considered to be the source of our life force and the animating factor in all living beings.

Chi is the bridge between the body and our consciousness. Because the body, Chi and consciousness or spirit are linked, a change in one may easily affect the other two. The mind leads and the Chi follows; the Chi leads and the body follows. Chi is the midpoint or interface between the body and mind. Directing the Chi enables us to make changes in both body and mind. Chi also binds things together. It is what keeps the constituents of our bodies from separating and dissipating. When the human body loses its breath of life, the original energy (life-force) leaves it, allowing the body to decompose.

Chi holds the organs, glands, blood vessels, and other bodily parts in place. When the body's Chi becomes weak, a loosening of the organs can occur in which they drop from their normal positions, leading to poor functioning and ill health. Chi also warms the body; any increase or decrease in bodily heat indicates the strength of its flow.

The Chi that forms the heavens and earth is essentially the same as the Chi that forms living beings. "God created man in His image." Human beings are a microcosm of the universe. Thus, Chi flows throughout the universe, and it also flows through humans. Through studying how our own Chi works, we can also understand the workings of the universe.

Movement of Chi

Chi circulates along acupuncture meridians or energy channels in the human body in a similar way that radio waves travel through space. These radiate to and resonate with all cells in the body. Although imperceptible, like radio waves, electricity moving faster than the speed of light continuously charges the body.
When this energy flow is unrestricted, the body harmonizes the flow to optimize body functioning. When we abuse or cause stress to our bodies, sometimes the stress is so intense or so constant that, in effect it "overloads" the circuit. The "circuit breaker" pops and needs to be reset before energy can flow properly.

The major meridians connect to one another deep inside the body. On the surface, the meridians circulate closely, within a half-inch to an inch of connecting with each other. Each meridian runs on both sides of the body--mirroring itself.

The Chinese were especially concerned with eliminating energy blockages in the energetic body channels. They created intricate maps of the body's energy system, and used acupuncture needles to draw awareness to specific areas where energy blockages occurred - rebalancing the channels.

Today we have learned how to accomplish this same balancing of the body's electromagnetic system in non-invasive ways, utilizing different mediums such as the hands, special magnets, crystals, reiki patterns, etc. The highest goal of inner alchemy is to transform our cells to unite with Cosmic Energy and become immortal cosmic cells of the universe.

In Chinese acupuncture anatomy, the internal organs of the body are all interconnected with one another by pathways called meridians, which are located throughout the body. The concept of these pathways could be compared with Western ideas of the blood vessels and capillaries, or the nervous system with its centers and peripheral branches. This system is not, however, the same as either of these other systems. The meridians, unlike the blood vessels, which can be seen with the naked eye, are not visible. As the blood vessels function as pathways for the blood, so the meridians are pathways in which energy is circulated throughout the body.

The meridians spread out through the entire body connecting all the tissues and organs of the body binding it together as an organic unit. Meridians are also referred to as Vessels, Chings, or Channels. The Qi consists of all essential life activities which include the spiritual, emotional, mental and the physical aspects of life. A person's health is influenced by the flow of Qi in the body, in combination with the universal forces of Yin and Yang. If the flow of Qi is insufficient, unbalanced or interrupted, Yin and Yang become unbalanced, and illness may occur.

The most important and essential ones for the circulation of Chi, and for most therapeutic applications are the twelve Primary Meridians and two Extra Vessels. These are :

1. Lung 2. Large Intestine
3. Brain 4. Spinal Cord
5. Heart 6. Small Intestine
7. Liver 8. Gall Bladder
9. Spleen 10. Stomach
11. Kidneys 12. Urinary Bladder

The two extra Meridians are the Conception Vessel and the Governing Vessel. (The term Conception Vessel does not imply that this Vessel is exclusively concerned with the female, although it does have extensive connections with the female reproductive system, and is frequently used in the treatment of gynecological disturbances. It is, however, present in both male and female).

These two Extra Vessels are usually included in a listing of the twelve Meridians, because of their importance in the circulation of energy, and their value in many treatment formularies. They also have their own acupuncture points.

In short, there are fourteen main meridians (12 Main Meridians, 1 front midline and 1 back midline) through which the energy flows in the body. Out of these, there are twelve organ Meridians, i.e. each Meridian is associated with one organ of the body. The Front Midline Yin (CV) and Back Middle Yang (GV) Meridians are associated with the organs that lie in the centre of the body (both on the front and the back). These 2 Meridians control the energy flow in all the meridians and correlate the activities.

However, the usual life phenomenon is undertaken by the 12 main meridians. As long as the 12 meridians normally work, the body maintains a healthy condition.

Supplied with energy through these 12 meridians, the functions of our body organs and tissues are carried out. If there is any disorder or imbalance in the flow of energy in these meridians, the body becomes sick. If this imbalance is restored, the body becomes healthy again.

When the energy supplied through 12 meridians becomes normal, the corresponding body organs resume their proper functioning and the disease is removed.

Some of the meridians of the body run in a more or less horizontal direction, while others run vertically. The twelve Primary Meridians are vertical channels.

The twelve Primary Meridians are also bilateral. This means they have symmetrical pathways on either side of the body in relation to the median (mid-line) of the body, just as we have a right and a left side. There is a Lung meridian on both the left side of the body and the right side of the body, and similarly with all of the other eleven Meridians. The acupuncture points for the various Meridians are in the same mirror image locations on either side of the body.

When we discuss Meridians, we will speak of them singularly to avoid confusion. If we mention the Heart Meridian, you may think of this meridian on either side of the body. As each side is identical, it is not necessary to discuss them both.

These meridians are as per Classical Acupuncture System. But we are not studying classical accupuncture. But our intention is to learn about Byol meridians. Similarly, as there are correspondence points of all body organs, meridians have also their corresponding meridians known as Byol meridians.

So our first step is to use seeds on these Byol meridians. So lelt us first understand where is their location on our hands and feet.

First of all, please note that functions of meridians are a lot more than functions of organs after which their names are given. Lung meridian has more functions than Lung as a organ. (To understand this, you can read our books Advance Sujok Therapy (Part 1 of 2) and Advance Sujok Therapy (Part 2 of 2)). Here we will take functions of Lung as a body organ.

Blood

The nutrients from food are digested by the Spleen and Stomach and they are then transported to the Heart and Lung and turned into red (oxygenated) blood by qi. The essence of Kidney produces bone marrow, and bone marrow uses the digested food to produce blood.

Qi of Kidney promotes digestion by Spleen, which in turn strengthens the Heart and Lung. This interaction therefore promotes haemopoesis.

There is a close relationship between qi and blood. The formation and circulation of blood depends on qi, whereas the formation and distribution of qi, as well as the health of the various organs of the body, is dependent on adequate nourishment from the blood. If the flow of blood 'stagnates' the circulation of qi is 'retarded' and, conversely, if the circulation of qi is 'retarded' then the blood flow 'stagnates'.

Body Fluid

Body fluid is formed from food and drink. It exists in the blood, the tissues, and all the body openings and cavities.

Location of Byol meridians on hands and feet

For treatment, first of all we should know the location of the Byol Meridians on the fingers/toes on Yin as well as on the Yang sides. As already given that Meridians are on both sides of the body, left and right, Byol meridians are also on both the hands/feet, left and right.

In earlier lessons you have seen that there are two types of correspondence points, that is, primary and secondary correspondence points. It was explained there that the primary correspondence point of any left organ would in the left hand and that its secondary correspondence point will be in the right hand, and so on. For example, we know Liver is on the right side of the body. Hence its primary correspondence point will be in the right hand, whereas the secondary correspondence point of Liver will be in the left hand. Primary Byol meridians of the right side of the body are in the Index Finger (2nd toe) and Middle Finger (3rd toe) of the right hand/foot, whereas the Secondary Byol meridians of the right side of the body are in the Small Finger (5th toe) and Ring Finger (4th toe) of the left hand/foot.

Primary Byol meridians of the left side of the body are in the Index Finger (2nd toe) and Middle Finger (3rd toe) of the left hand/foot, whereas the Secondary Byol meridians of the left side of the body are in the Small Finger (5th toe) and Ring Finger (4th toe) of the right hand/foot.

Abbreviations used for meridians :

A : Lung B : LI
I : Brain J : SC
E : Heart F : SI
L : Liver K : GB
D : Spleen C : Stomach
H : Kidney G : UB

Fig. 146 explain as to how the Primary Yin meridians are located on the Index Finger and Middle Finger, and how the Secondary Yin meridians are placed on the Little Finger and Ring Finger of Left and Right Hands.

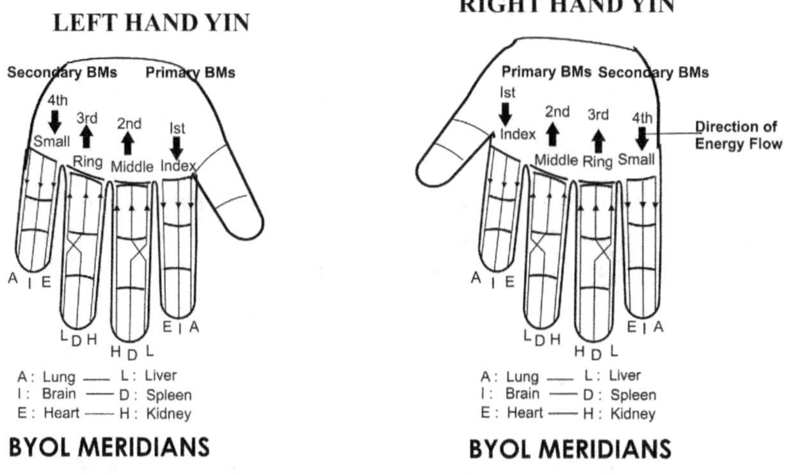

Fig. 146

Fig. 147 explains as to how the Primary Yang meridians are located on the Index Finger and Middle Finger, and how the Secondary Yang meridians are placed on the Little Finger and Ring Finger of Left and Right Hands.

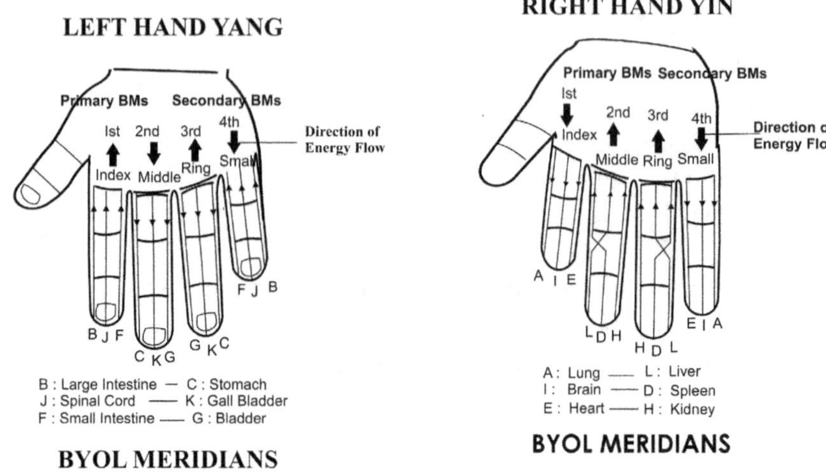

Fig. 147

Fig. 148 explains as to how the Primary Yin meridians are located on the 2nd toe and 3rd toe, and how the Secondary Yin meridians are placed on the 5th toe and 4th toe of the Left and Right Toes.

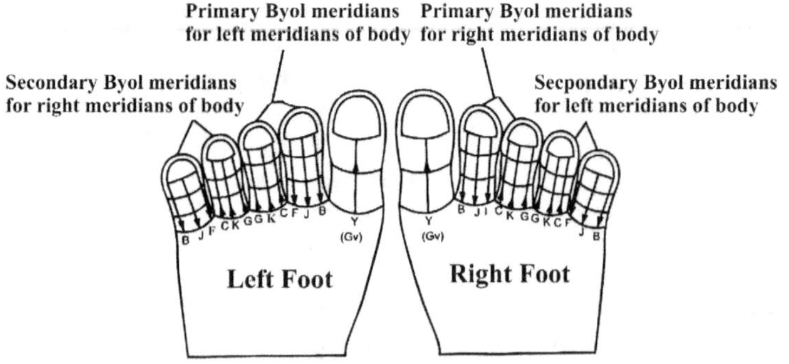

Location of Primary and Secondary meidians on feet - Yang

Fig. 148

Fig. 148a explains as to how the Primary Yang meridians are located on the 2nd toe and 3rd toe, and how the Secondary Yang meridians are placed on the 5th toe and 4th toe.

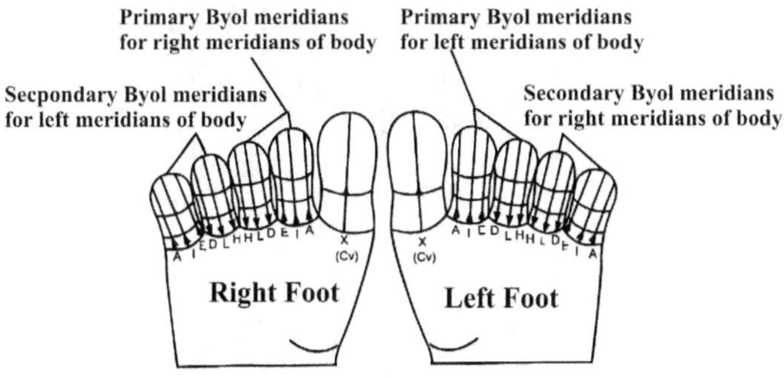

Location of Primary and Secondary meidians on feet - Yin

Fig. 148a

To locate Byol meridians, a centerline has been drawn on the Yin and Yang sides of each finger/toe respectively and then additional two parallel lines have been drawn at the same distance from each centerline. Now there are total six Byol meridians at the same interval on the Index Finger (2nd toe) and Middle finger (3rd toe) receptively - three on the Yin side and 3 on the Yang side.

Please note that the Liver Byol meridian and the Spleen Byol meridian intersect at the middle of the 2nd bar of the Yin area of the middle finger/toe, as shown in the above Fig. 149.

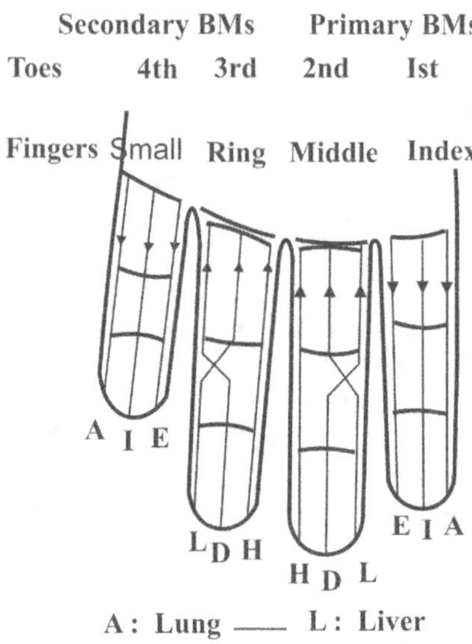

A : Lung ——— L : Liver
I : Brain ——— D : Spleen
E : Heart ——— H : Kidney

Location of BYOL MERIDIANS (Yin side)

Fig. 149

Conception Vessel (Fig 150) and Governor Vessel (Fig 150a and Fig 150b) are represented on Yin and Yang sides of thumb.

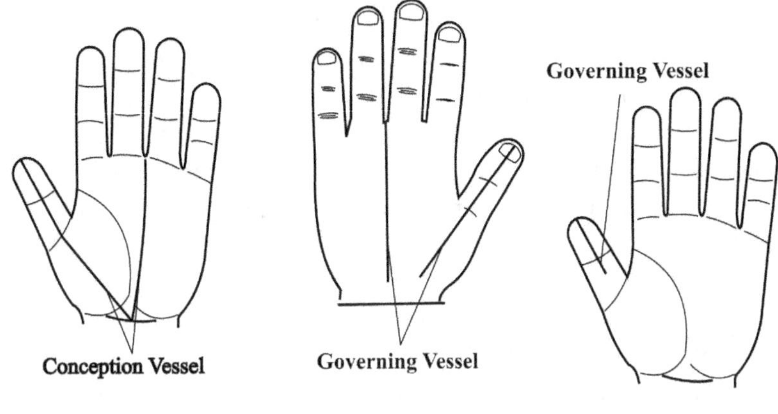

Fig. 150

When there is excessive flow of energy in a meridian, it is called excessive and when there is deficient flow of energy in a meridian, it is called deficiency. As explained above, this excessiveness or deficiency causes diseases in the body.

Please note that meridians on yin side of hand are called Yin Meridians and meridians on yang side of hand are called Yang Meridians. In fact, these meridians (say, Yin or Yang organs of the body associated with these meridians) are always in an imbalance state, that is, these are either excessive or deficient. However, a little exceeding or lacking is regarded as normal state as it does not bring any disorder in the body. But if this imbalance is quite pronounced, it produces a disorder in the body. To cure, treatment of these meridians has to be done. It is done either by tonifying or sedating the concerned Byol Meridian. By tonifying or sedating, a balance has to be created in the flow of energy, which will produce a curative effect in the body. It is simple to understand that when a meridian is excessive, it should be sedated, and that when a meridian is deficient, it should be tonified to produce the curative effect.

This is done through use of seeds on the meridians. In Sujok Therapy there are other many methods. But here we would limit ourselves to the use of seeds.

To understand how to use, we should know two things : direction of energy flow in the Byol meridian and direction of energy flow of a seed.

Direction of the Energy Flow in the Meridians
Since it is the flow of energy in the meridians which is to be controlled, we should know the direction of flow of energy.

In the Yang area of the body, there are three Yang meridians, such as, Large Intestine meridian, Spinal Cord meridian and Small Intestine meridian from the end of the hand through the arm, and there are three Yang meridians, such as Stomach meridian, Gall Bladder meridian and Urinary Bladder meridian along the Yang area of leg towards the end of the foot. Fig. 151

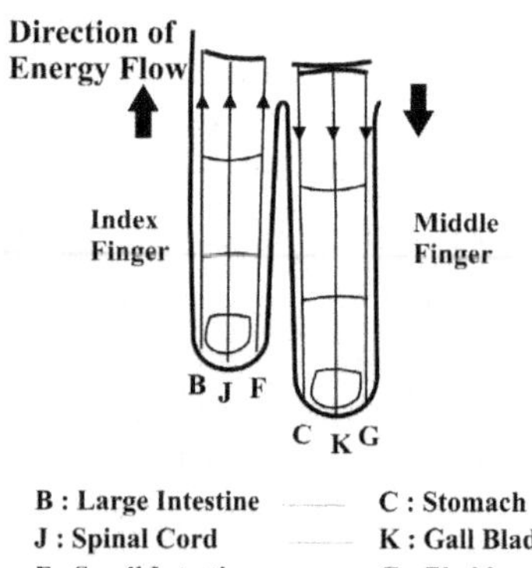

**DIRECTION OF ENERGY
FLOW : YANG SIDE**

Fig. 151

In the Yin area of the body, there are three Yin meridians, such as, Liver meridian, Spleen meridian and Kidney meridian along the Yin area of the leg from the end of the foot, and there are three meridians, such as, Lung meridian, Brain meridian and Heart meridian from the Yin area of the arm towards the end of the hand. Fig. 152

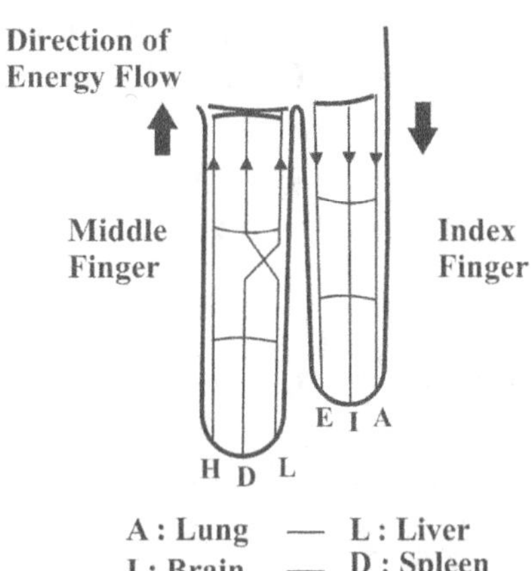

**DIRECTION OF ENERGY
FLOW: YIN SIDE**

Fig. 152

Index Finger (2nd Toe) and the Middle Finger (3rd Toe) are the Main Byol Meridians, whereas the Ring Finger (4th toe) and Little Finger (5th toe) are the Secondary Byol Meridian.

Energy flow for Primary Yin Meridian in the Index Finger (2nd toe) flows out and the energy flow for the Primary Yin Meridian in the Middle Finger (3rd Toe) flows in.

The energy flow for Primary Yang Meridians in the Index Finger (2nd toe) flows in and the energy flow for the Yang Meridians in the Middle Finger (3rd Toe) flows out.

The energy flow for Secondary Yin Meridians in the Little Finger (5th toe) flows out and the energy flow for the Secondary Yin Meridians in the Ring Finger (4th Toe) flows in.

The energy flow for Secondary Yang Meridians in the Little Finger (5th toe) flows in and the energy flow for the Secondary Yang Meridians in the Ring Finger (4th Toe) flows out.

After having understood the direction of flow of energy in all the meridians, let us now understand the direction of flow of energy in a seed.

Direction of energy flow of a seed

Direction of energy flow in a seed is shown in Fig. 153. You would note that the energy flows from the top core of the seed to down as shown.

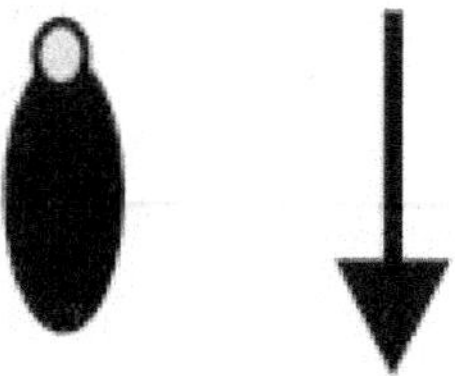

Fig. 153

So if you want to tonify a Byol meridian, affix the seed on the Byol meridian in such a way that it matches with the energy flow of the meridian.

Example: Tonification of Kidney Meridian (Fig. 154)

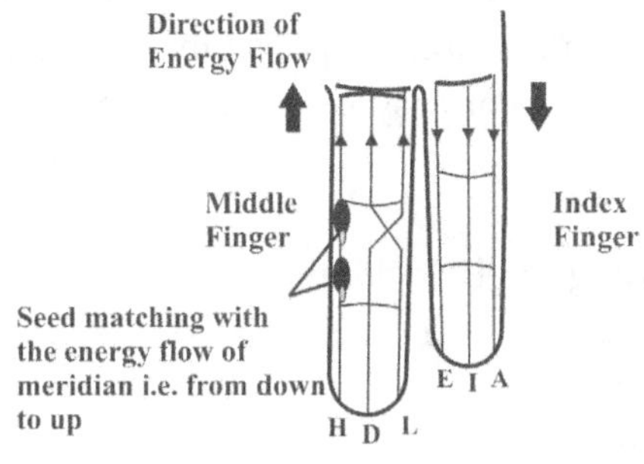

TONIFICATION OF KIDNEY MERIDIAN USING SEED

Fig. 154

Example: Sedation of Kidney Meridian (Fig. 155)

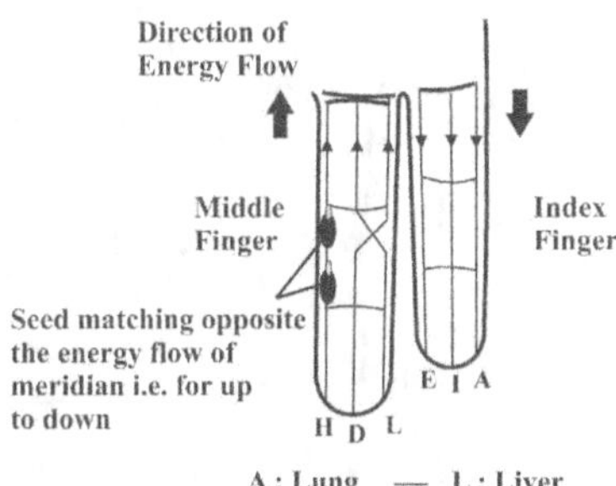

SEDATION OF KIDNEY MERIDIAN USING SEED

Fig. 155

Another Method

Yin-Yang Way :

As the name implies, in this way, tonification/sedation of Yin-Yang pair of the Byol Meridian is done, taking Yin and Yang pair Byol Meridian as one Meridian. For easy reference, these pairs are once again below :

Yin Byol Meridian Yang Byol Meridian :

Lung B : Large Intestine
I : Brain J : Spinal Cord
E : Heart F : S Intestine
L : Liver G : Gall Bladder
D : Spleen C : Stomach
H: Kidney K : Urinary Bladder
Conception Vessel Governor Vessel

Sedation of Stomach will result in tonification of Spleen, as shown in Fig 156.

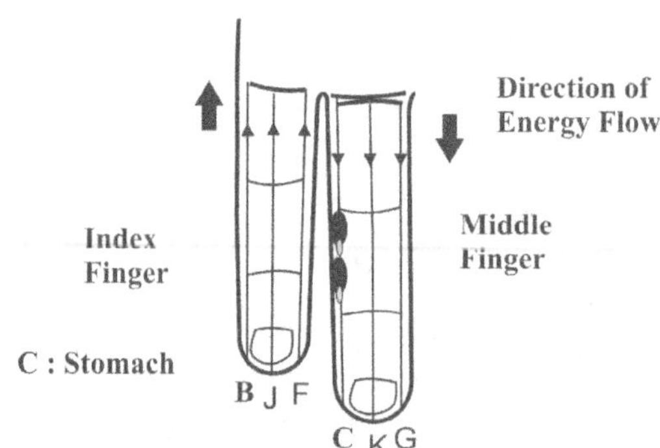

Tonification of Spleen through Sedation of Stomach BM : Left Hand : Yang Side

Fig. 156

See, in the picture above, Energy Flow in the Stomach meridian is downward and we are using seeds with their energy flow upwards. Hence, sedation of Stomach. If Stomach is sedated, automatically Spleen will be tonified.

The Byol Meridian Tonification/Sedation Diagnosis

When a disease has attacked, tonify or sedate a particular Byol Meridian. This is the Byol Meridian Tonification/Sedation Diagnosis.

But how to judge whether to tonify or sedate a particular meridian. As a first resort do whatever you think, that is, do one thing, either tonify or sedate and then observe the reaction. For example when a patient has a bad cough, try sedating his/her Lung Byol meridian. If it results in even worse, diagnose that the patient's Lung meridian is deficient. Why, because it means this cough comes from Lung deficiency. As the Lung Byol has been sedated in that situation, it is adjudged that the Lung meridian has become more deficient and the cough has got worse. Hence, in case of Lung deficiency, sedating makes the patient get worse. This shows that tonification of the Lung meridian will be better in this case and cough will become less.

Similarly, the opposite is also possible. Suppose, as a first resort you do the tonification in this case and the result is worsening of the cough. It means this cough comes from excessiveness of Lung meridian and by tonification we are increasing it, resulting in worsening of cough. This shows that sedating of Lung meridian will be better in this case and cough will become less.

It is only for the beginners. Later with sufficient practice you will be able to diagnose whether the cough is from deficiency or excessiveness and treat the patient in a better manner.

The following will help you in deciding which meridian should be taken for treatment.

Yin-Yang Diagnosis : It is very important (though not always easy) to categorize symptoms into Yin-Yang categories. You have read something about Ying and Yang in Lesson 1.

It is important to consider the followings :

a. **How acute is the symptom?** If the symptoms are acute, and clear, it belongs to Yang. When symptoms are slight and not vivid, it is probably Yin. Yang is strong and Yin is weak.

b. **Is the process general or local?** : It means whether the symptoms are on the entire body, i.e. General, or located on some part of the body, i.e. Local. General symptoms belong to Yin, Local to Yang. For example, itching all over the body is Yin, itching of one localized part is Yang.

c. **Are symptoms predictable, repeatable?** : If the symptoms appear or aggravate at a certain time of day or night, or under certain known conditions, Yin energy prevails. That is, the symptoms are predictable. Yang energy shows itself unexpectedly, unpredictably, as episodes, not cycles.

d. **Duration of the process** : Chronic, long term cases belong to Yin. Acute, short term diseases are Yang. New disease that just began also most probably Yang.

e. **Location of the diseased organ?** : If the diseased part is on outer part, it belongs to Yang; if on inner part, it belongs to Yin. Skin belongs to Yang, internal organs to Yin. Upper part is Yang, lower is Yin. Right side for man is Yin, for woman is Yang. Left side for man is Yang, for woman is Yin.

CHAPTER TEN

SIX KI THEORY

The Six Ki Theory explains that there are six types of Ki on each meridian (Energies that flow in all that exists on the Universe) which affect our body, mind and soul. Any imbalance in these Ki and the result is some disorder in the body. So long as there is harmony and balance between these Six Ki, we remain healthy and when this harmony is disturbed, disease develops.

The Six Ki are : Wind, Heat, Hotness, Humidity, Dryness and Coldness.

There is nothing in this Universe which is beyond the scope of these Six Ki. Anything created is due to interaction between Six Ki and anything destructed is due to interaction between Six Ki. E.g. there is no life on the Sun due to an imbalance of Six Ki : Heat and Wind Ki dominate. There is also no life on the Moon, as the disharmony of Six Ki is caused by the absence of Wind energy. When there is no harmony, there can be no life. On the earth the Six Ki are balanced and thus, human beings may exist.

Once we know the general characteristics of each individual Six Ki, it is easy to understand which Ki is dominating, which Ki is lacking and what will be its result. E.g. if Wind Energy is lacking, it is easy to interpret that movement will be blocked. From the name of the energy itself, meaning is clear.

Each of the Six Ki has different characteristics and their functions are explained latter. (Please note that each Six Ki is associated with one of the Five Elements, Emotions, Reasons, etc and interacts with other Six Ki according to the Five Elements Principles : Creation, Subjugation, Anti-subjugation, and Anti-creation functions. You can read about this in our books Advance Sujok Therapy (Part of 2) and Advance Sujok Therapy (Part 2 of 2)).

Here we would limit ourselves to characteristics of Ki's and their functions and understand the use of seeds for treatment as per their functions.

Influence of Six Ki on the Earth can be understood by the cycle of seasons.

Wind is associated with Spring. Wind blows away earlier Coldness/Winter. Friction of Wind blowing causes heat.

Heat is associated with Summer. Heat caused by friction continues.

Hotness is associated with Summer. Changes into full Summer.

Humidity is associated with Monsoon. At saturation point of Humidity, rain comes.

Dryness is associated with Fall. After rains, the heat goes and it gets cool. A state of dryness. Trees/plants begin to fall.

Coldness is associated with Winter.

Again Wind. This cycle repeats itself continuously. The above weather conception of Six Ki is true for a certain standard region of the Earth, where the Six Ki are evenly distributed and the time lengths of every season are equal. But in different regions of the

Earth, the Six Ki are distributed unevenly. Seasons are different in time length during the yearly cycle.

Thus, in anything on this Universe, we can see the influence of Six Ki individually and the interaction of Six Ki among themselves.

As dominance of one Ki results into one weather condition, the dominance of one Ki in one region of the earth may result into one kind of diseases, and so on. For example, in Russia the Coldness Ki is excessive, so coldness diseases dominate in Russia. In India Heat and Hotness energies dominate - so there are more Heat and Hotness diseases.

Similarly, in the human bodies, the dominance of one or more Ki results into a particular constitution of the body and makes the body prone to certain diseases.

Characteristics of Six Ki

To understand the above, we should understand the general characteristics of all the Six Ki. Each of the Six Ki has its own characteristics, as hereunder :

1. Wind : It has no colour, noise or smell. It is movement energy. As every change, every process starts with a movement, Wind energy characterises a beginning of any change or event. It is associated with Spring, as Spring means freedom from confinement of coldness and ability to move is there.

All disease start from Wind; so it would give useful results if Wind energy of the diseased organ is treated first of all, to start the process of restoration of health.

Wind is associated with Wood of the Five Elements.

It is also associated with Spring season of the year, Muscle System of the body, birth as part of the life cycle, Anger as an Emotion, Originality as a Reason activity, East and Southeast as Directions, Green colour, Sour taste, Numbers 3 and 8, etc. (All these are described in detail in our earlier books on Advance and Master Sujok Therapy).

When Wind comes, it shakes everything, blows away the Humidity, and brings with it thunder and lightening. Similarly, when a person is affected by Wind energy, his spirit loses concentration and the body becomes light like hair. As the Wind penetrates, the Muscle system becomes affected, Anger dominates and loss of spiritual stability appears.

Wind subjugates Humidity, but is subjugated by Dryness. Wind also anti-subjugates Dryness.

Wind does not blow by itself. It is just one of the Six Ki co-existing in a complicated relationship with other Six Ki.

In the Six Ki cycle of circulation Wind comes after Coldness and creates Heat.

There are two types of Wind energy : Yin Wind and Yang Wind.

When the Wind is mild, predictable, expected during Spring or forecasted during a particular season, it belongs to Yin Wind. When the gust of wind is strong, unpredictable, short in duration (like a typhoon or tornado), it belongs to Yang Wind.

Yin Wind energy is associated with the Liver meridian and Yang Wind energy with the Gall Bladder meridian.

2. Heat : In the Six Ki cycle of circulation, Heat comes after Wind and creates Hotness.

Heat is aggressive in its nature as Yang and causes warming up and expansion. It prevents contraction. According to the subjugation principle, Heat subjugates Dryness; Heat anti-subjugates Coldness and is subjugated by Coldness energy.

It is associated with the Fire of the Five Elements. It is also associated with Summer as season of the year, Circulation System (Heart and Blood Vessels) of the body, Growth as part of life cycle, Joy as an Emotion, Desire as a Reason activity, South as a Direction, Bitter taste, and Red colour, etc.

With Heat increasing, all organs of the body become active. Movement becomes fast and active, plants and animals grow fast and vigorous in warm weather. Heat causes a feeling of Joy and a strong Desire to carry out action.

If a human being is affected by Heat, he becomes willing to do only what he wants to do. His sense of judgement is weakened He is unable to use his mind properly. At the same time he becomes ambitious and vigorous. His body may generate heat and show inflammation.

There are two types of Heat energy : Yin Heat and Yang Heat.

When Heat is not strong and predictable, it belongs to Yin Heat.

When Heat is strong, unpredictable or short in duration, it belongs to Yang Heat.

For example, the Sun belongs to Yang Heat, when we emphasize on the strong heat, but on the other hand it belongs to the Yin Heat because it supplies continuous heat energy to living things on earth.

Yin Heat is associated with the Heart meridian and Yang Heat with the Small Intestine meridian.

3. Hotness : Hotness energy comes after Heat in the Six Ki circulation cycle and creates Humidity.

Continuous Heat for a long time results into Hotness. Hotness corresponds to the stage of maturity. Hotness is the climax of Yang - a point when full growth and ripeness is achieved. All living things have to reach the Hotness stage to become a harmonized organism of maturity.

Hotness is associated with the Fire of the Five Elements, Late Summer as season of the year, Nervous System of the body, full growth as a part of life cycle, Happiness as Emotion, Ambition as Reason activity, South in Direction, Bitter taste, and Orange colour (for light), etc.

Hotness subjugates Dryness and anti-subjugates Coldness, but is subjugated by Coldness.

If a human being is affected by Hotness, symptoms like sweating, thirstiness, hotness, unpleasant feeling, loss of power and full of gas appear. Excessive Hotness leads to a loss of will power, laziness prevails. Happiness subdues Sadness on an emotion level.

There are two types of Hotness : Yin Hotness and Yang Hotness.

When Hotness is constant, predictable, it is Yin Hotness.

When it is strong, short and temporary, it is Yang Hotness.

Yin Hotness energy is associated with the Brain meridian and Yang

Hotness with the Spinal Cord meridian.

4. Humidity : Humidity comes after Hotness and creates Dryness. Humidity is the Six Ki which dominates during the rainy season in late summer. Humidity is the turning point, where decline starts in the Six Ki circulation cycle.

Humidity subjugates Coldness as water gradually melts ice, it is subjugated by Wind and sometimes anti-subjugated by Coldness.

It is associated with the rainy season, when everything becomes full of dampness, rivers overflow. Wetness is absorbed and shows itself as swelling.

Humidity is associated with the Earth of the Five Elements, Monsoon as season of the year, Flesh (Fat and Lymph) of the body, prosperity as part of the life cycle, Agony as an Emotion, Consciousness (thinking) as a Reason activity, Centre as a direction, Sweet taste, and Yellow colour, etc.

When affected by Humidity, a human body feels heaviness and tiredness, no desire to move, the fat layer increases. The feeling of the pain starts at the Humidity stage (dull pain).

During Humidity, itching is one of the main symptoms. Some of the bodily functions seem to be impaired at this stage in a similar way.

If Humidity is excessive, Worry and Agony is the result. Mental and spiritual activities reach their peak at the Humidity stage.

There are two types of Humidity : Yin Humidity and Yang Humidity.

Constant, predictable humidity belong to Yin Humidity.

Short, temporary, strong humidity belongs to Yang Humidity.

In our body Yin Humidity is associated with Spleen meridian and Yang Humidity with the Stomach meridian.

5. Dryness : Dryness comes after Humidity and creates Coldness. Dryness subjugates Wind, but it anti-subjugates Heat/Hotness and is subjugated by Heat or Hotness.

It is associated with the Metal of the Five Elements.

Dryness is also associated with Fall as season of the year, Skin and Hairs of the body, atrophy as part of the life cycle, Sadness as an Emotion, Will as a Reason activity, West, and White Colour, etc.

When affected by Dryness, the following symptoms may appear in the body : rough skin, xeroderma (skin becomes dry and forms bran-like scales), sclerosis, loss of weight, wrinkles, gray hair, menopause in women. Pain caused by Dryness is strong but tolerable, not continuous and more intense than during the Humidity stage.

There are two types of Dryness : Yin Dryness and Yang Dryness.

Frequent, constant and predictable Dryness belongs to Yin Dryness.

Temporary, acute and extreme dryness belongs to Yang Dryness.

Yin Dryness energy is associated with the Lung meridian and Yang Dryness with the Large Intestine meridian.

6. Coldness : Coldness comes after Dryness. Coldness subjugates Heat or Hotness and is subjugated by Humidity, sometimes it anti-subjugates Humidity.

It is the Final stage of a disease and such ailments as cancer, chronic ulcer, sclerosis, diseases of the aged are all Coldness symptoms. Everything hard or cold in the body belongs to Coldness.

Coldness belongs to the Water as one of the Five Elements.

It is associated with Winter as season of the year, Bones of the body, old age or death as part of the life cycle, Fear as an Emotion, Wisdom as Reason activity, North as a direction, Salty taste, and Black colour, etc.

There are two types of coldness: Yin Coldness and Yang Coldness.

Repeated, predictable, long-term coldness is Yin coldness.

Sudden, strong, temporary appearing coldness is Yang Coldness.

Yin Coldness energy is associated with the Kidney meridian, Yang Coldness with the Urinary Bladder meridian.

The Life Cycle From The Six Ki Perspective

To understand the Six Ki a little bit more, let us understand its influence on the life cycle of a human being. Various age groups are characterized by different Energies, as given hereunder :

Wind Energy is associated with the Age group 1-10 years.
As during this period Wind energy dominates, children between this age groups are always moving, they cannot sit idle, their movements are quick, almost constant. It is difficult for them to

concentrate and be attentive on one subject for long. Unpredictable moods, fits of anger, now weeping then laughing, loud, noisy and curious.

Heat Energy is associated with the Age group 11-20 years.
Children of 11-20 years (adolescents) show Heat excessiveness. They like to laugh and talk. They are full of ambitions, great expectations for the future. They have many unrealized desires.

Hotness Energy is associated with the Age group 21-30 years.
Hotness characterises full maturity. Hence, during this age, the physical body reaches full maturity. All parts of the body are formed; Emotional capacity also blooms, and Reason activity is also in full. During this period desires are realized in practice, the human being may reach harmony and happiness.

Humidity Energy is associated with the Age group 31-40 years.
Humidity characterises less movement. Hence, during this age there is a tendency to move less, internal organs also slow down; hence, basic metabolism also decreases; and weight gain is there. At this age people concentrate and work hard but worry about their friends, children and loved ones. Thinking prevails and spiritual prosperity may be reached.

Dryness Energy is associated with the Age group 41-50 years.
Dryness Energy is characterized by Autumn, fall of leaves, etc. Similarly, due to hormonal changes, tissues of the body lose their tendency to water retention, and body weight decreases. The skin becomes dry, wrinkles appear. Also, since Dryness is associated with atrophy, the functions of the body organs decline. This period is associated with Sadness, as one thinks of good old times when one was full of energy and desire. If unsuccessful, Sadness continues and results in Depression.

Coldness Energy is associated with the Age group 51 years onward.

Coldness relates to old age, when the person becomes wiser and is cautious and calculative. Either all the desires have been fulfilled or lost, & little energy is left for any new desire. Hence, there is little desire. There may be a fear of impending death. During this period, physical power is lost.

Body temperature decreases and illnesses of Coldness prevail (stones, strokes, infarction, cancer, etc.)

This life cycle of age groups may be flexible according to the region, races and countries where they are living.

CHAPTER ELEVEN

SIX KI THEORY (Contd)

Location of Six Ki Points on the Meridians

As explained above, any disease/disorder, whether at the physical, mental or spiritual level, is the result of an imbalance in these Six Ki. Sometimes one Ki is dominant; then its characteristics dominate in the disease/disorder; sometimes more than one Ki are dominant. The treatment process involves removing this imbalance in these Six Ki.

For Six Ki treatment, it is imperative to know the exact location of each Six Ki point on the Byol Meridians on the fingers. We already know where the Byol Meridians are located on our fingers/toes. Let us now understand the exact location of Six Ki on the BMs.

Figs. 157, 158 clearly show the location of Six Ki points on the fingers on Yin as well as on the Yang sides.
The sequence of Six Ki points located on Yin Byol Meridians (from distal to proximal point) is as follows :

First Point : Wind
Second Point : Heat (or Hotness)
Third Point : Humidity
Fourth Point : Dryness
Fifth Point : Coldness

The sequence of Six Ki points located on Yang Byol Meridians (from distal to proximal point) is as follows:

First Point : Dryness
Second Point : Coldness
Third Point : Wind
Fourth Point : Heat (or Hotness)
Fifth Point : Humidity

5 (6) points on each Byol Meridian; hence, there are 60 Six Ki points located on Yin and Yang Byol Meridians used for metaphysical treatment.

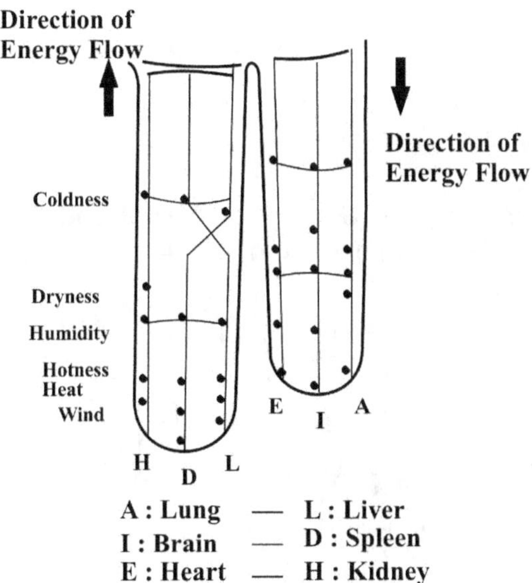

Yin Side

Fig. 157

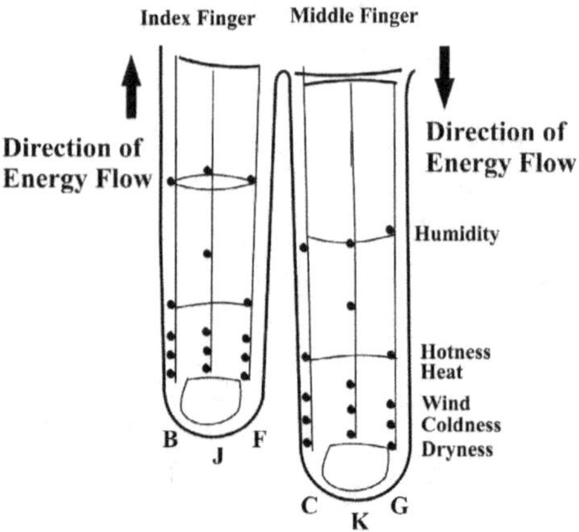

B : Large Intestine   C : Stomach
J : Spinal Cord   K : Gall Bladder
F : Small Intestine   G : U Bladder

YANG SIDE

Fig. 158

Six Ki points on the Conception Vessel and Governor Vessel Meridians (Fig. 159 and Fig. 160)

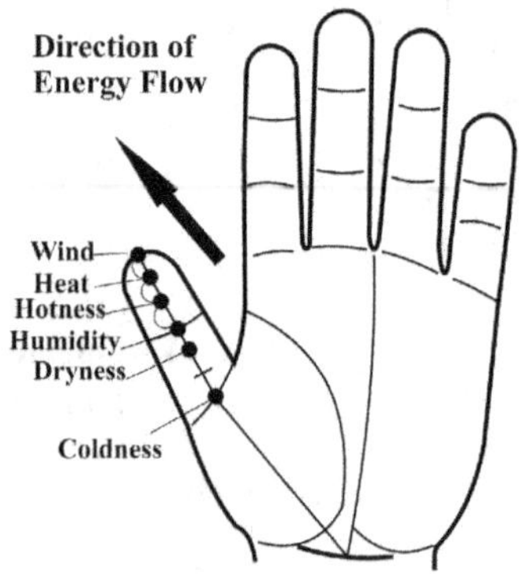

Six Ki Pionts on the Conception Vessel BM

Fig. 159

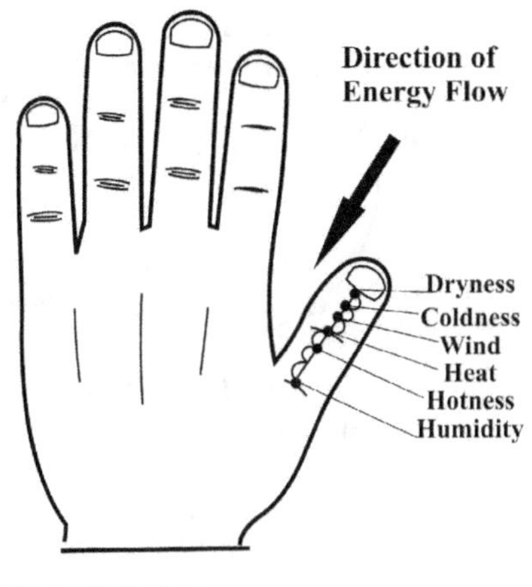

**Six Ki Points on
Governor Vessel BM**

Fig. 160

Functions of Six Ki:
Following are the four functions of Six Ki (these functions are true
to all associations of six ki, e.g. emotions, reasons, elements, sense
organs, etc, details of which are given in our course : MD Sujok), i.e.
Creation, Anti-creation, Subjugation and Anti-subjugation. Here it
is limited to Seed Therapy.

The Creation Cycle of Six-Ki can be taken as under :

Creation Cycle of Six Ki : (Fig.161) The image shows :

Wind creates Heat/Hotness
Heat/Hotness creates Humidity
Humidity creates Dryness.
Dryness creates Coldness, and

Coldness creates Wind

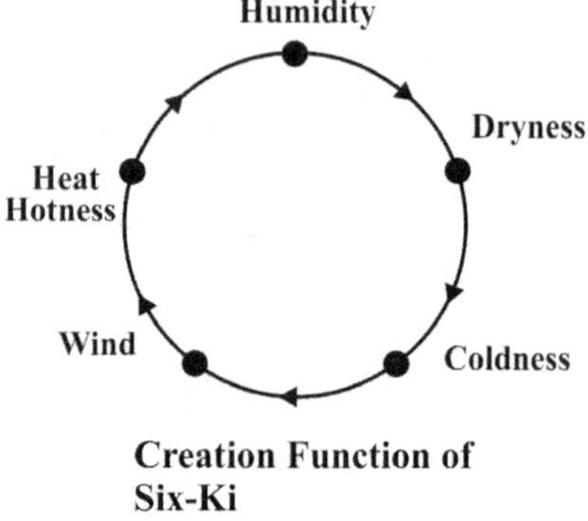

**Creation Function of
Six-Ki**

Fig. 161

From the above figure, we find that Heat/Hotness is created by
Wind. Hence, Wind is the Mother of Heat/Hotness and Heat/
Hotness is the Son of Wind. Similarly, Wind is the Son of Coldness
and Coldness is the Mother of Wind. And so on.

Anti-Creation Cyle of Six-Ki : Fig. 162

It cultivates order consciousness and leads to an existence of
voluntary autonomy in the universe. It gives rise to altruistic
conceptions, produces the spirit of law obedience, and law
observance, loyalty to ones country, filial piety for parents, etc.

For example, it is natural that parents love their children; it is
Creation function. But when children love their parents, it is Anti-
creation function. When a company takes care of its employees, the
employees in turn take care of the company. This is Anti-creation
function.

Wind anticreates Coldness. (Wind affects Coldness not directly, but indirectly through the Humidity : Wind is strong and subjugates Humidity; hence, Humidity becomes weak and it does not have enough strength to subjugate Coldness; in this way Coldness gains power. As a result Wind as a Son anti-creates Coldness as a Mother.) Similarly, this function can be understood for all other Six Ki.

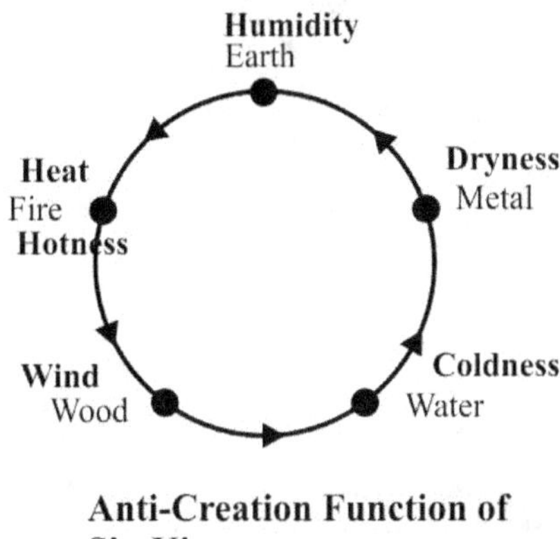

Anti-Creation Function of Six-Ki

Fig. 162

Subjugation Cycle of Six-Ki : Fig 163
It is a very powerful and quick acting interaction between the Six Ki.

Fig. 163 would clarify this function of Six Ki :

Wind subjugates Humidity
Humidity subjugates Coldness
Coldness subjugates Heat/Hotness,
Heat/Hotness subjugates Dryness, and
Dryness subjugates Wind

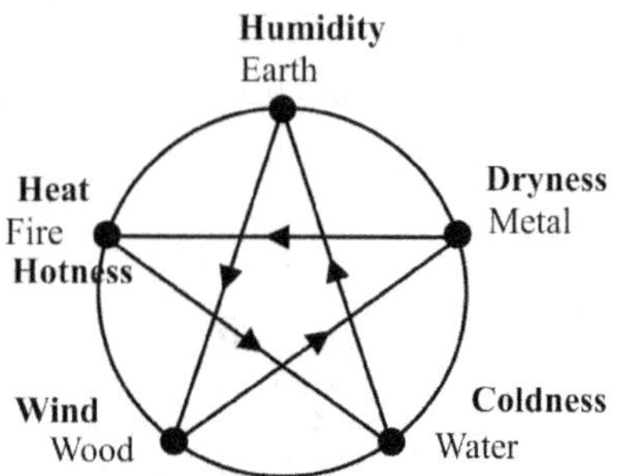

**Anti-Subjugation Function
of Six-Ki**

Fig. 163

As already said, it is a very important function. Without this function, there may be anarchy; there will be no check on the Creation Function. For example, all laws, army, police, etc. subjugate the society for its protection. Eating is subjugating, as it means killing (animals, plants, grains, etc). Similarly, in our body, all organs try to subjugate others and in this struggle, create a balance between them. If at any time one organ becomes weak and is being subjugated by the other organ, the result is disorder in the body. To cure, a balance has to be achieved in Six Ki/Five Elements (as a result, in the organs associated with these Six Ki/ Five Elements).

Creation is Yin, being slow, continuous, gradual process. Subjugation is Yang, being fast, strongly acting process.

Anti-subjugation Cycle of Six-Ki : Fig 164

Examples of anti-subjugation are : protest against a dictator, resistence against corruption, revision of old laws, a growth to a new stage or order, etc.

All of the four actions between the Six Ki/Five Elements take place simultaneously and the power of an Six Ki/Element is determined by all other Six Ki/Elements.

Wind antisubjugates Dryness
Dryness antisubjugates Heat/Hotness
Heat/Hotness antisubjugates Coldness
Coldness antisubjugates Humidity
Humidity antisubjugates Wind

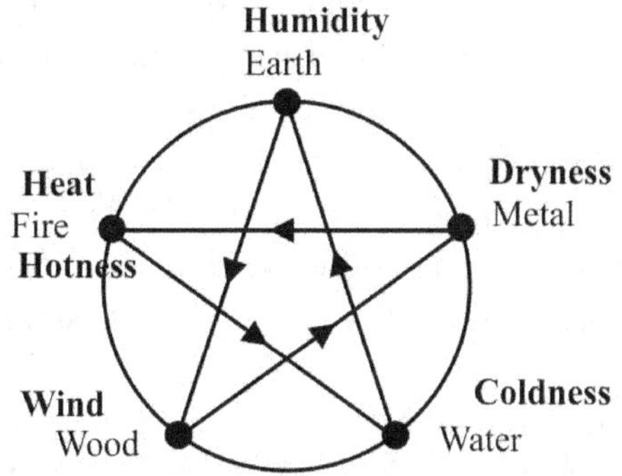

**Anti-Subjugation Function
of Six-Ki**

Fig. 164

The Six Ki Treatment

The Six Ki treatment is a metaphysical method of Su Jok Therapy. The treatment is carried out using the Six Ki points on Byol Meridian in hands and feet.

In the 12 meridians, the Six Ki (Energy) such as Wind, Heat, Hotness, Humidity, Dryness and Coldness are flowing with themselves divided into Yin and Yang. Hence, diseases maybe cured by utilizing the diagnosis resulting from the Six Ki situation. This is called the Six-Ki Byol Meridian Tonification/Sedation method.

It is imperative to learn to interpret each disease/disorder in terms of Six Ki categories. That is why the general characteristics of each Six Ki have been given. After categorising the disease/disorder in terms of Six Ki, an individual treatment formulae is made.

Treatment of Six Ki points is done by tonification, that is, increasing the energy of the point, or sedation, that is, decreasing the energy of the points. Tonification is done when a Six Ki point is deficient and sedation is done when a Six Ki point is excessive.

We have studied the properties of Six Ki. Heart energy produces heat. If it is excessive, it will give heat-related problems, like high fever, rash, redness, inflammation, etc. Then sedation is required. Similarly if Humidity is excessive, there will be swelling, soft tumours etc. then also sedation is required. So many symptoms of six ki have been given to understand whether tonification or sedation is required.

Let me give you some more hints in diagnosing a disorder through Six Ki properties.

Analysing symptoms based on Six Ki categories : Each Energy has certain characteristic symptoms. These are being given hereunder, to help diagnose:

Wind :

Symptoms of Wind Energy : Wind energy is connected with muscle system. Muscles have a complex structure : long muscles, the muscle tissue itself is Yin, and ligaments - short and strong, located near joints are Yang. That is why in cases of diseases of the joints (and ligaments) Yang Wind (Gall Bladder Wind) tonification or sedation should be done for good results.

Pain is not characteristic of Wind energy. One of the symptoms of Wind energy is itching as a initial stage.
If there is not enough muscle power or problems with muscle contraction, we should also consider Wind energy. A person with well developed muscle system points to Yin Wind excessiveness. For instance, while walking a patient gets muscle cramps. Walking belongs to Yin Wind energy. If walking provokes muscle spasms, the patient probably has Wind excessiveness. Yin Wind subjugates Yin Humidity and Yin Humidity cannot subjugate Yin Coldness, as a consequence, Yin Coldness becomes excessive. (Spasms belong to Coldness Six Ki).

Or, for example, the patient has arthritis, it is hard for him to move. Joints may be viewed as moving joints. To produce movement strong contractions of muscles and ligaments are necessary. Strong movement is connected with Yang Wind of Gall Bladder. As he is unable to walk, this case may be viewed as Yang Wind deficiency and Yang Wind (Gall Bladder Wind) tonification is prescribed to elevate the symptoms.

Heat :

Symptoms based on Heat Energy : Heat energy is connected to Blood Vessels System. Pain is not characteristic of Heat energy.

The blood vessel system as a whole belongs to Yin Heat category, but diseases of the Arteries belong to Yang Heat of the Small Intestine and diseases of Veins - to Yin Heat of the Heart (for example, varicose veins are a manifestation of Yin Heat (Heart Heat) deficiency.

Heat energy corresponds to red colour. If the patient has red spots on the skin all over the body (large part of the skin is affected), it points to Yin Heat excessiveness. If only the face or one part of the body's skin manifests red coloring, or the patient becomes red unpredictably, it points to Yang Heat excessiveness.

Menstruating in women is connected to Yang Heat, but when it comes to periodical, it becomes Yin Heat.

High temperature is connected to Yin Heat of the Heart, high fever - to Yang Heat of the Small Intestine.

Hotness :

Symptoms based on Hotness Energy : Connected to the Nervous System in our body. Pain is not characteristic of this energy.

Symptoms of Hotness are : thirst, sweating, apathy, discomfort, lazy feeling, a feeling of expanding, hardness of breathing, feeling of hotness and producing gas. Psychiatric diseases are often connected to Hotness energy (the Brain and Spinal Cord meridians).

Often some symptoms which cannot be categorized in particular Six Ki, belong to Hotness Energy category.

Hotness is metaphysical Six Ki, so it has leading position among others.

Humidity:

Symptoms based on Humidity Energy : Connected with Flesh, Fat tissue and the Lymphatic System of the body.

A dull pain is characteristic of Humidity. Itching comes from deep within (not superficial as for Wind energy manifestation).

A feeling of heaviness, no desire to move, just sit or lie down for a while. The body becomes blotted, fat tissue - excessive.

There is an excessiveness of liquids in all body systems, which can be seen at a glance. A patient that has been fat or fleshy from childhood belongs to Yin Humidity (Spleen Humidity) excessiveness, a patient who gained weight quickly and unexpectedly is an example of Yang Humidity (Stomach Humidity) excessiveness.

As the Lymphatic System belongs to Humidity category, all diseases of the Lymphatic Vessels and nodes may be treated by tonifying or sedating Yin or Yang Humidity (depending on each individual case). In some cases, where there is an inflammation of lymph nodes, Spleen Humidity sedation of original Six Ki treatment gives excellent results. Or Spleen Heat sedation of branch Six Ki treatment can be used with good results.

Dryness :

Symptoms based on Dryness Energy : Connected with Skin and Hair of our body.

Since Dryness energy belongs to the same category as skin and hair of our body components and is connected with such symptoms of processes as atrophy, sclerosis, benign tumours, menopause. Sharp pain is characteristic of Dryness (neurological pain, as a dry, crumbled leaf). Sometimes severe itchiness is a manifestation of Dryness energy.

If patient is slim, Yin Dryness of the Lung is in excess. If a patient lost a considerable amount of weight in a short period of time, it could most probably be caused by Yang Dryness excessiveness of the Large Intestine. Dryness excessiveness manifests itself in organ malfunction, which is often connected to organic damage.

Coldness :

Symptoms based on Coldness Energy : Connected to Bones of our body. Pain as a manifestation of Coldness excessiveness, is very strong, continuous and intense. If the patient's body is cold to touch, Yin Coldness (Kidney Coldness) dominates. If a feeling of coldness appears from time to time unpredictably, Yang Coldness of the Bladder is excessive. When Yin Coldness is excessive, cold showers (Yang Coldness) can be of great help by Yang -Yin principle. Coldness can be described by hardening and high density. Sclerosis, cirrhosis, tumours, gall bladder or kidney stones - all belong to Coldness category.

Trauma, bone fractures, accidents and acute diseases that endanger life (heart stroke) are all manifestation of Yang Coldness.

The most important part of Six Ki diagnosis is to correctly categorize the symptoms. It is very important to remember about the protective (immune) reactions of the body. Before attempting to categorize any symptom, the practitioner should understand the disease phenomena and underlying causes for each symptom. For instance a person who was exposed to coldness and as a consequence fever appears. In this case Yang Heat energy protects the body from the excessive amount of Yang Coldness and Yang Heat tonification (and not sedation) is recommended to restore balance. Also, Yang Coldness sedation could bring a good result.

Let us examine another example.

When a patient goes outside in cold weather his nose gets watery. Yang Humidity protects the body from Yang Coldness excessiveness. If the body is not protected by Yang Humidity, Yang Coldness shall penetrate the body and enter the Lungs. In this case, Lung Humidity should not be sedated, but on the contrary, tonified, which would prevent Lung Coldness.

Use of Seeds: Treatment through Six Ki Tonification/Sedation

We have studied that there are Six Ki points on each meridian. So whatever Six Ki point you want to tonify or sedate, apply seed on it with a surgical tape.

As already said, for better results professional knowledge about seeds, their properties, etc is required. But for a layman, you can use the seeds as explained in the earlier lessons, i.e. by direction, by shape, by properties, etc. and also latter by Six Ki methods.

TREATMENT FORMULAE

Based on the functions of Six Ki, as explained above, following formulae have been derived for treatment of various diseases. The following tables are given as a reference table for Original Six Ki Treatment formulae, Branch Six Ki and Super Six Ki formulae.

ORIGINAL SIX KI FORMULAE (Fig. 165)

Lungs Dryness Sedation
Lungs Dryness Sedation
Heart Heat Tonification
Kidney Coldness Sedation
Brain Dryness Sedation
Lungs Dryness Tonification
Lungs Dryness Tonification
Heart Heat Sedation
Kidney Coldness Tonification
Brain Dryness Tonification

Large Intestine (LI) Dryness Sedation
LI Dryness Sedation
SI Heat Tonification
UB Coldness Sedation
SC Dryness Sedation
LI Dryness Tonification
LI Dryness Tonification
SI Heat Sedation
UB Coldness Tonification
SC Dryness Tonification

Heart Heat Sedation
Heart Heat Sedation
Kidney Coldness Tonification
Spleen Humidity Sedation
Brain Heat Sedation
Heart Heat Tonification

Heart Heart Tonification
Kidney Coldness Sedation
Spleen Humidity Tonification
Brain Heat Tonification

SI Heat Sedation
SI Heat Sedation
UB Coldness Tonification
Stomach Humidity Sedation
Spinal Cord Heat Sedation
SI Heat Tonification
SI Heat Tonification
UB Coldness Sedation
Stomach Humidity Tonification
SC Heat Tonification

Spleen Humidity Sedation
Spleen Humidity Sedation
Liver Wind Tonification
Lungs Dryness Sedation
Brain Humidity Sedation
Spleen Humidity Tonification
Spleen Humidity Tonification
Liver Wind Sedation
Lungs Dryness Tonification
Brain Humidity Tonification

Fig. 166

Stomach Humidity Sedation
Stomach Humidity Sedation
GB Wind Tonification
LI Dryness Sedation
SC Humidity Sedation
Stomach Humidity Tonification

Stomach Humidity Tonification
GB Wind Sedation
LI Dryness Tonification
SC Humidity Tonification

Kidney Coldness Sedation
Kidney Coldness Sedation
Spleen Humidity Tonification
Liver Wind Sedation
Brain Coldness Sedation
Kidney Coldness Tonification
Kidney Coldness Tonification
Spleen Humidity Sedation
Liver Wind Tonification
Brain Coldness Tonification

UB Coldness Sedation
UB Coldness Sedation
Stomach Humidity Tonification
GB Wind Sedation
SC Coldness Sedation
UB Coldness Tonification
UB Coldness Tonification
Stomach Humidity Sedation
GB Wind Tonification
SC Coldness Tonification

Liver Wind Sedation
Liver Wind Sedation
Lungs Dryness Tonification
Heart Heat Sedation
Brain Wind Sedation
Liver Wind Tonification
Liver Wind Tonification
Lungs Dryness Sedation

Heart Heat Tonification
Brain Wind Tonification

GB Wind Sedation
GB Wind Sedation
LI Dryness Tonification
SI Heat Sedation
SC Wind Sedation
GB Wind Tonification
GB Wind Tonification
LI Dryness Sedation
SI Heat Tonification
SC Wind Tonification

Brain Hotness Sedation
Brain Hotness Sedation
Kidney Coldness Tonification
Spleen Humidity Sedation
Brain Hotness Tonification
Brain Hotness Tonification
Kidney Coldness Sedation
Spleen Humidity Tonification

SC Hotness Sedation
SC Hotness Sedation
UB Coldness Tonification
Stomach Humidity Sedation
SC Hotness Tonification
SC Hotness Tonification
UB Coldness Sedation
Stomach Humidity Tonification

BRANCH SIX KI TREATMENT FORMULAE (Fig. 167)

Lungs Dryness Sedation
Lungs Dryness Sedation
Lungs Heat Tonification
Lungs Coldness Sedation
Brain Dryness Sedation
CV Dryness Sedation
Lungs Dryness Tonification
Lungs Dryness Tonification
Lungs Heat Sedation
Lungs Coldness Tonification
Brain Dryness Tonification
CV Dryness Tonification

LI Dryness Sedation
LI Dryness Sedation
LI Heat Tonification
LI Coldness Sedation
SC Dryness Sedation
GV Dryness Sedation
LI Dryness Tonification
LI Dryness Tonification
LI Heat Sedation
LI Coldness Tonification
SC Dryness Tonification
GV Dryness Tonification

Heart Heat Sedation
Heart Heat Sedation
Heart Coldness Tonification
Heart Humidity Sedation
Brain Heat Sedation
CV Heat Sedation
Heart Heat Tonification

Heart Heat Tonification
Heart Coldness Sedation
Heart Humidity Tonification
Brain Heat Tonification
CV Heat Tonification

SI Heat Sedation
SI Heat Sedation
SI Coldness Tonification
SI Humidity Sedation
SC Heat Sedation
GV Heat Sedation
SI Heat Tnification
SI Heat Tonification
SI Coldness Sedation
SI Humidity Tonification
SC Heat Tonification
GV Heat Tonification

Spleen Humidity Sedation
Spleen Humidity Sedation
Spleen Wind Tonification
Spleen Dryness Sedation
Brain Humidity Sedation
CV Humidity Sedation
Spleen Humidity Tonification
Spleen Humidity Tonification
Spleen Wind Sedation
Spleen Dryness Tonification
Brain Humidity Tonification
CV Humidity Tonification

Stomach Humidity Sedation
Stomach Humidity Sedation

Stomach Wind Tonification
Stomach Dryness Sedation
SC Humidity Sedation
GV Humidity Sedation
Stomach Humidity Tonification
Stomach Humidity Tonification
Stomach Wind Sedation
Stomach Dryness Tonification
SC Humidity Tonification
GV Humidity Tonification

Fig. 168

Kidney Coldness Sedation
Kidney Coldness Sedation
Kidney Humidity Tonification
Kidney Wind Sedation
Brain Coldness Sedation
CV Coldness Sedation
Kidney Coldness Tonification
Kidney Coldness Tonification
Kidney Humidity Sedation
Kidney Wind Tonification
Brain Coldness Tonification
CV Coldness Tonification

UB Coldness Sedation
UB Coldness Sedation
UB Humidity Tonification
UB Wind Sedation
SC Coldness Sedation
GV Coldness Sedation
UB Coldness Tonification
UB Coldness Tonification
UB Humidity Sedaastion

UB Wind Tonification
SC Coldness Tonification
GV Coldness Tonification

Liver Wind Sedation
Liver Wind Sedation
Liver Dryness Tonification
Liver Heat Sedation
Brain Wind Sedation
CV Wind Sedation
Liver Wind Tonification
Liver Wind Tonification
Liver Dryness Sedation
Liver Heat Tonification
Brain Wind Tonification
CV Wind Tonification

GB Wind Sedation
GB Wind Sedation
GB Dryness Tonification
GB Heat Sedation
SC Wind Sedation
GV Wind Sedation
GB Wind Tonification
GB Wind Tonification
GB Dryness Sedation
GB Heat Tonification
SC Wind Tonification
GV Wind Tonification

Brain Hotness Sedation
Brain Hotness Sedation
Brain Coldness Tonification
Brain Humidity Sedation
CV Humidity Sedation

Brain Hotness Tonification
Brain Hotness Tonification
Brain Coldness Sedation
Brain Humidity Tonification
CV Humidity Tonification

SC Hotness Sedation
SC Hotness Sedation
SC Coldness Tonification
SC Humidity Sedation
GV Humidity Sedation
SC Hotness Tonification
SC Hotness Tonification
SC Coldness Sedation
SC Humidity Tonification
GV Humidity Tonification

SUPER SIX KI TREATMENT FORMULAE (Fig. 169)

Lungs Dryness Sedation
Lungs Dryness Sedation
Heart Heat Tonification
Lungs Heat Tonification
Kidney Coldness Sedation
Lungs Coldness Sedation
Brain Dryness Sedation
CV Dryness Sedation
Lungs Dryness Tonification
Lungs Dryness Tonification
Heart Heat Sedation
Lungs Heat Sedation
Kidney Coldness Tonification
Lungs Coldness Tonification
Brain Dryness Tonification

CV Dryness Tonification

LI Dryness Sedation
LI Dryness Sedation
SI Heat Tonification
LI Heat Tonification
UB Coldness Sedation
LI Coldness Sedation
SC Dryness Sedation
GV Dryness Sedation
LI Dryness Tonification
LI Dryness Tonification
SI Heat Sedation
LI Heat Sedation
UB Coldness Tonification
LI Coldness Tonification
SC Dryness Tonification
GV Dryness Tonification

Fig. 170

Heart Heat Sedation
Heart Heat Sedation
Kidney Coldness Tonification
Heart Coldness Tonification
Spleen Humidity Sedation
Heart Humidity Sedation
Brain Heat Sedation
CV Heat Sedation
Heart Heat Tonification
Heart Heat Tonification
Kidney Coldness Sedation
Heart Coldness Sedation
Spleen Humidity Tonification
Heart Humidity Tonification

Brain Heat Tonification
CV Heat Tonification

SI Heat Sedation
SI Heat Sedation
UB Coldness Tonification
SI Coldness Tonification
Stomach Humidity Sedation
SI Humidity Sedation
SC Heat Sedation
CV Heat Sedation
SI Heat Tonification
SI Heat Tonification
UB Coldness Sedation
SI Coldness Sedation
Stomach Humidity Tonification
SI Humidity Tonification
SC Heat Tonification
CV Heat Tonification

Spleen Humidity Sedation
Spleen Humidity Sedation
Liver Wind Tonification
Spleen Wind Tonification
Lungs Dryness Sedation
Spleen Dryness Sedation
Brain Humidity Sedation
CV Humidity Sedation
Spleen Humidity Tonification
Spleen Humidity Tonification
Liver Wind Sedation
Spleen Wind Sedation
Lungs Dryness Tonification
Spleen Dryness Tonification
Brain Humidity Tonification

CV Humidity Tonification

Fig. 171

Stomach Humidity Sedation
Stomach Humidity Sedation
GB Wind Tonification
Stomach Wind Tonification
LI Dryness Sedation
Stomach Dryness Sedation
SC Humidity Sedation
GV Humidity Sedation
Stomach Humidity Tonification
Stomach Humidity Tonification
GB Wind Sedation
Stomach Wind Sedation
LI Dryness Tonification
Stomach Dryness Tonification
SC Humidity Tonification
GV Humidity Tonification

Kidney Coldness Sedation
Kidney Coldness Sedation
Spleen Humidity Tonification
Kidney Humidity Tonification
Liver Wind Sedation
Kidney Wind Sedation
Brain Coldness Sedation
CV Coldness Sedation
Kidney Coldness Tonification
Kidney Coldness Tonification
Spleen Humidity Sedation
Kidney Humidity Sedation
Liver Wind Tonification
Kidney Wind Tonification

Brain Coldness Tonification
CV Coldness Tonification

UB Coldness Sedation
UB Coldness Sedation
Stomach Humidity Tonification
UB Humidity Tonification
GB Wind Sedation
UB Wind Sedation
SC Coldness Sedation
GV Coldness Sedation
UB Coldness Tonification
UB Coldness Tonification
Stomach Humidity Sedation
UB Humidity Sedation
GB Wind Tonification
UB Wind Tonification
SC Coldness Tonification
GV Coldness Tonification

Liver Wind Sedation
Liver Wind Sedation
Lungs Dryness Tonification
Liver Dryness Tonification
Heart Heat Sedation
Liver Heat Sedation
Brain Wind Sedation
CV Wind Sedation
Liver Wind Tonification
Liver Wind Tonification
Lungs Dryness Sedation
Liver Dryness Sedation
Heart Heat Tonification
Liver Heat Tonification
Brain Wind Tonification

CV Wind Tonification

GB Wind Sedation
GB Wind Sedation
LI Dryness Tonification
GB Dryness Tonification
SI Heat Sedation
GB Heat Sedation
SC Wind Sedation
GV Wind Sedation
GB Wind Tonification
GB Wind Tonification
LI Dryness Sedation
GB Dryness Sedation
SI Heat Tonification
GB Heat Tonification
SC Wind Tonification
GV Wind Tonification

Brain Hotness Sedation
Brain Hotness Sedation
Kidney Coldness Tonification
Brain Coldness Tonification
Spleen Humidity Sedation
Brain Humidity Sedation
CV Hotness Sedation
Brain Hotness Tonification
Brain Hotness Tonification
Kidney Coldness Sedation
Brain Coldness Sedation
Spleen Humidity Tonification
Brain Humidity Tonification
CV Hotness Tonification

SC Hotness Sedation

SC Hotness Sedation
UB Coldness Tonification
SC Coldness Tonification
Stomach Humidity Sedation
SC Humidity Sedation
GV Hotness Sedation
SC Hotness Tonification
SC Hotness Tonification
UB Coldness Sedation
SC Coldness Sedation
Stomach Humidity Tonification
SC Humidity Tonification
GV Hotness Tonification

Please remember the above methods of treatment are universal for all levels : Six Ki (Emotions or Reasons Treatment levels- not covered here. For more details on this, please read our books Advance Sujok Therapy (Part 1 of 2) and Advance Sujok Therapy (Part 2 of 2).

CHAPTER TWELVE

APPLICATION OF SIX KI THEORY

Application of seeds as per Six Ki Theory

You have already studied the Six Ki theory, their association with seasons, life cycle, their characteristics. Six Ki theory is given above in detail. How to use it with seeds has already been explained.

See the following info. It gives you the Ki, associated colour and associated seeds. You can search for more.

Ki (Energy) Colour Seeds

Wind Green Pumpkin, Sunflower, Coriander, Fennel, Pea, Lentil, Lemon, Fennel

Heat Red Pomegranate, Capsicum, Carrot, Red Radish, Red Pepper, Beetroot

Hotness Orange Capsicum, Marigold Flower, Carrot

Humidity Yellow Capsicum, Mustard, Strawberry, Lentil

Dryness Brown Buckwheat, Cumin, Mustard, Linseed, Flax, Coriander, Ajwain, Celery, hazelnuts, dates, cedar, buckthorn, burdock, barley, Fenugreek

Coldness Blue Blue Pumpkin seeds, Cotton seeds

Brightness White Melon, Sesame, White Radish, White Beetroot

Blackness Black Sesame, Mustard, Chie, Kalonji, Black Cumin,

Now first of all recall the location of Ki points on Yin and Yang meridians, Fig 172 and Fig/ 173.

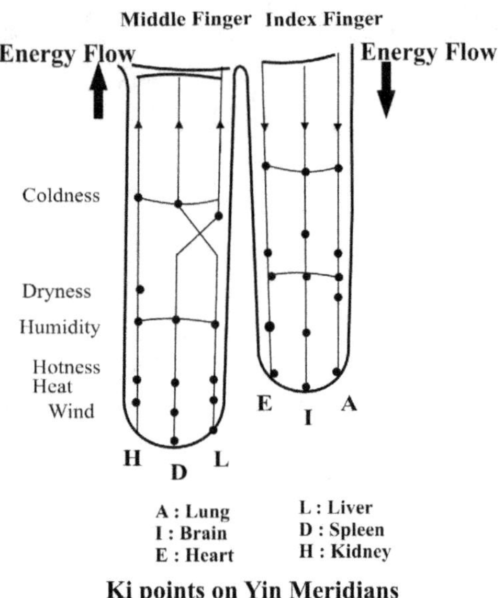

Ki points on Yin Meridians

Fig. 172

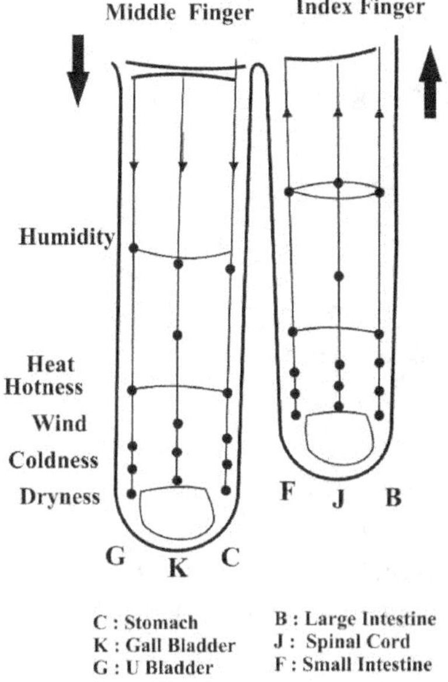

Ki points on Yang meridians

Fig. 173

Also please note that wherever I have written "put red dot" on a particular meridian, it means you have to put the same color seed on it.

For knowing the seeds colours, please refer to the table above.

Please keep in mind that to become perfect in Seed Therapy, you should have a lot of knowledge about plants and seeds. You can take the help of an expert gardener in this regard. However, we have given you sufficient hints to practise seed therapy. I have given above a table which tells you the name of colours of different seeds as per Six Ki. Actually you need to know only 6 seed colours (as per Six Ki Theory) and only 8 seed colours (as per Eight Ki Theory).

Treatment formulae and Examples

Original Six Ki: Yin organs

Lung Dryness Sedation:

Lung Dryness sedation
ii. Heart Heat tonification
iii. Kidney Coldness sedation
iv. Brain Dryness sedation

i. Lung Dryness Sedation : Then see the colour of energy, that is Dryness in this case. Colour of Dryness is White. Since we want to sedate it, we use colour Red, as Heat subjugates Dryness. So we put Red dot on the Lung Dryness point. Fig. 174

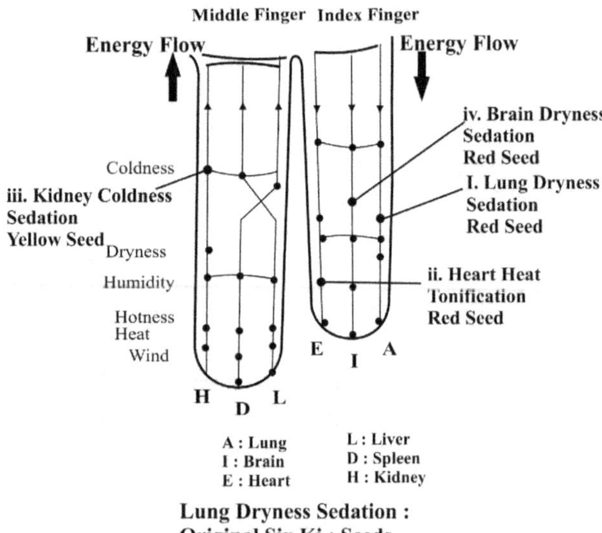

Lung Dryness Sedation :
Original Six Ki : Seeds

Fig. 174

ii. Heart Heat Tonification : Then see the colour of next energy, that is Heat in this case. Colour of Heat is Red. Since we want to tonify it, we use colour Red. So we put Red dot on the Heart Heat point.

iii. Kidney Coldness sedation : Then see the colour of next energy, that is Coldness in this case. Colour of Coldness is Black. Since we want to sedate it, we use colour Yellow (as Humidity subjugates Coldness and the colour of Humidity is Yellow). So we put Yellow dot on the Kidney Coldness point.

iv. Brain Dryness Sedation : Then see the colour of next energy, that is Dryness in this case. Colour Dryness is White. Since we want to sedate it, we use colour Red (as Heat subjugates Dryness and the colour of Heat is Red). So we put Red dot on the Brain Dryness point.

Original Six Ki : Yang Organs

LI Dryness Sedation Fig 175

i. LI Dryness sedation
ii. SI Heat tonification
iii. UB Coldness sedation
iv. Spinal Cord Dryness sedation

i. LI Dryness sedation : See the colour of energy, that is Dryness in this case. Colour of Dryness is White. Since we want to sedate it, we use colour Red, as Heat subjugates Dryness. So we put Red dot on the LI Dryness point. Fig 175

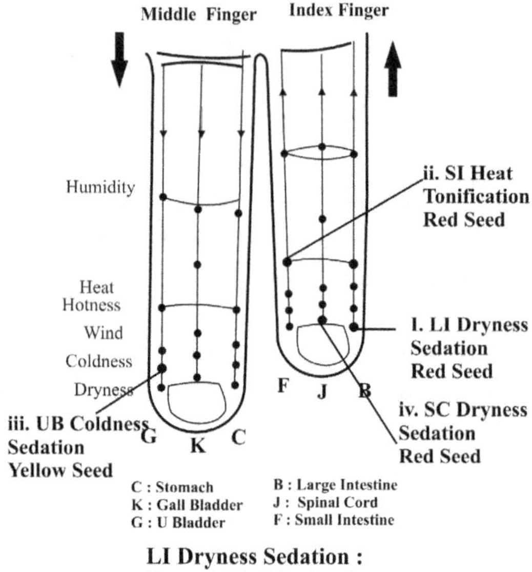

**LI Dryness Sedation :
Branch Six Ki : Seeds**

Fig. 175

ii. SI Heat tonification : Then see the colour of next energy, that is Heat in this case. Colour of Heat is Red. Since we want to tonify it, we use colour Red. So we put Red dot on the SI Heat point.

iii. UB Coldness sedation : Then see the colour of next energy, that is Coldness in this case. Colour of Coldness is Black. Since we want to sedate it, we use colour Yellow (as Humidity subjugates Coldness and the colour of Humidity is Yellow). So we put Yellow dot on the UB Coldness point.

iv. Spinal Cord Dryness sedation: Then see the colour of next energy, that is Dryness in this case. Colour Dryness is White. Since we want to sedate it, we use colour Red (as Heat subjugates Dryness and the colour of Heat is Red). So we put Red dot on the Spinal Cord Dryness point.

Branch Six Ki : Yin organs

Lungs Dryness Sedation Fig 176

i. Lung Dryness Sedation
ii. Lung Heat Tonification
iii. Lung Coldness Sedation
iv. Brain Dryness Sedation
v. CV Dryness Sedation

i. Lung Dryness Sedation : See the colour of energy, that is Dryness in this case. Colour of Dryness is White. Since we want to sedate it, we use colour Red, as Heat subjugates Dryness. So we put Red dot on the Lung Dryness point.

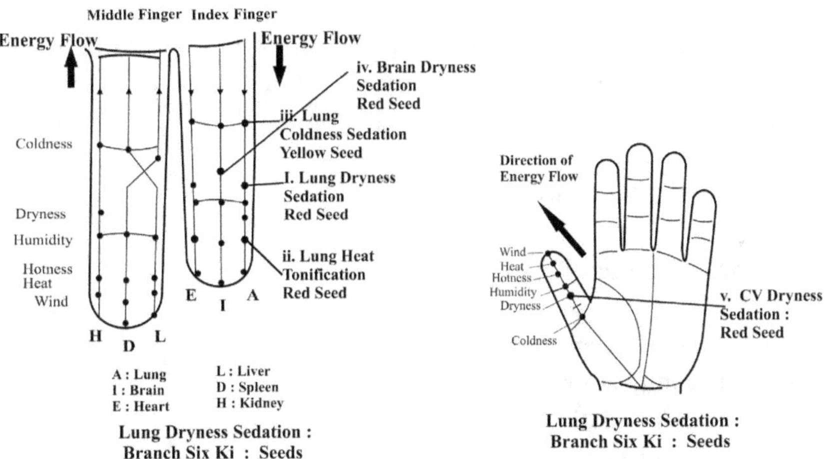

A : Lung
I : Brain
E : Heart
L : Liver
D : Spleen
H : Kidney

**Lung Dryness Sedation :
Branch Six Ki : Seeds**

**Lung Dryness Sedation :
Branch Six Ki : Seeds**

Fig. 176

ii. Lung Heat Tonification : Then see the colour of next energy, that is Heat in this case. Colour of Heat is Red. Since we want to tonification it, we use colour Red, as Heat subjugates Dryness. So we put Red dot on the Lung Heat point.

iii. Lung Coldness Sedation : Then see the colour of next energy, that is Coldness in this case. Colour of Coldness is Black. Since we want to sedate it, we use colour Yellow, as Humidity subjugates Coldness and colour of Humidity is Yellow. So we put Yellow dot on the Lung Coldness point.

iv. Brain Dryness Sedation :Then see the colour of next energy, that is Dryness in this case. Colour Dryness is White. Since we want to sedate it, we use colour Red (as Heat subjugates Dryness and the colour of Heat is Red). So we put Red dot on the Brain Dryness point.

v. CV Dryness Sedation : Then see the colour of next energy, that is Dryness in this case. Colour Dryness is White. Since we want to sedate it, we use colour Red (as Heat subjugates Dryness and the colour of Heat is Red). So we put Red dot on the CV Dryness point.

Branch Six Ki : Yang organs

LI Dryness Sedation Fig 177

i. LI Dryness Sedation
ii. LI Heat Tonification
iii. LI Coldness Sedation
iv. Spinal Cord Dryness Sedation
v. GV Dryness Sedation

i. LI Dryness Sedation : Then see the colour of energy, that is Dryness in this case. Colour of Dryness is White. Since we want to sedate it, we use colour Red, as Heat subjugates Dryness. So we put red dot on the LI Dryness point. Fig 177

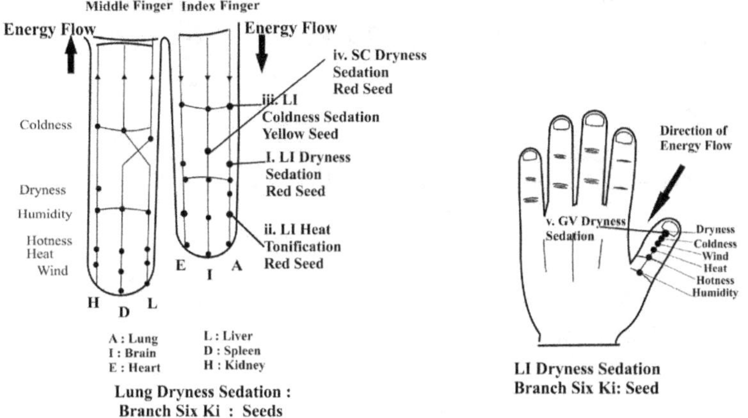

Fig. 177

ii. LI Heat Tonification : Then see the colour of energy, that is Heat in this case. Colour of Heat is Red. Since we want to tonification it, we use colour Red, as Heat subjugates Dryness. So we put red dot on the LI Heat point.

iii. LI Coldness Sedation : Then see the colour of energy, that is Coldness in this case. Colour of Coldness is Black. Since we want to sedate it, we use colour Yellow, as Humidity subjugates Coldness and colour of Humidity is Yellow. So we put Yellow dot on the LI Coldness point.

iv. SC Dryness Sedation : Then see the colour of next energy, that is Dryness in this case. Colour Dryness is White. Since we want to sedate it, we use colour Red (as Heat subjugates Dryness and the colour of Heat is Red). So we put Red dot on the Spinal Cord Dryness point.

v. GV Dryness Sedation: Then see the colour of next energy, that is Dryness in this case. Colour Dryness is White. Since we want to sedate it, we use colour Red (as Heat subjugates Dryness and the colour of Heat is Red). So we put Red dot on the GV Dryness point.

Super Six Ki : Yin Organs

Lungs Dryness Sedation Fig 178

i. Lung Dryness Sedation
ii. Heart Heat Tonification
iii. Lung Heat Tonification
iv. Kidney Coldness Sedation
v. Lung Coldness Sedation
vi. Brain Dryness Sedation
vii. CV Dryness Sedation

i. Lung Dryness Sedation : Then see the colour of energy, that is Dryness in this case. Colour of Dryness is White. Since we want to sedate it, we use colour Red, as Heat subjugates Dryness. So we put red dot on the Lung Dryness point.

ii. Heart Heat Tonification : Then see the colour of next energy, that is Heat in this case. Colour of Heat is Red. Since we want to tonify it, we use colour Red. So we put Red dot on the Heart Heat point.

iii. Lung Heat Tonification : Then see the colour of energy, that is Heat in this case. Colour of Heat is Red. Since we want to tonification it, we use colour Red, as Heat subjugates Dryness. So we put red dot on the Lung Heat point.

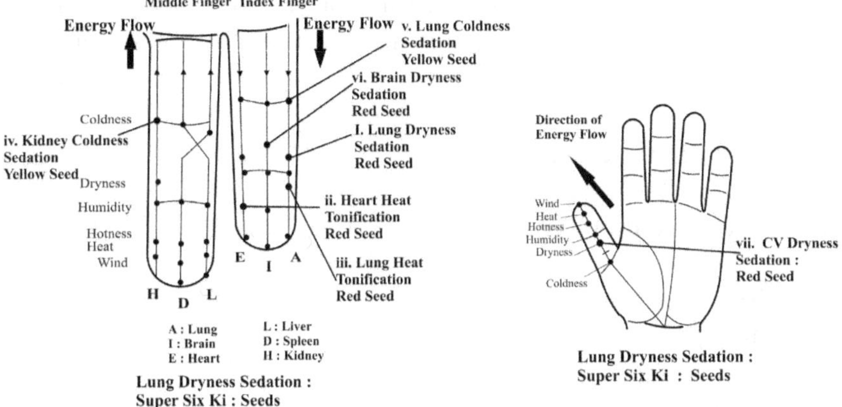

Fig. 178

iv. Kidney Coldness Sedation : Then see the colour of next energy, that is Coldness in this case. Colour of Coldness is Black. Since we want to sedate it, we use colour Yellow (as Humidity subjugates Coldness and the colour of Humidity is Yellow). So we put Black dot on the Kidney Coldness point.

v. Lung Coldness Sedation : Then see the colour of next energy, that is Coldness. Colour of Coldness is Black. Since we want to sedate it, we use colour Yellow (as Humidity subjugates Coldness and the colour of Humidity is Yellow). So we put Yellow dot on the Lung Coldness point.

vi. Brain Dryness Sedation : Then see the colour of next energy, that is Dryness in this case. Colour Dryness is White. Since we want to sedate it, we use colour Red (as Heat subjugates Dryness and the colour of Heat is Red). So we put Red dot on the Brain Dryness point.

vii. CV Dryness Sedation : Then see the colour of next energy, that is Dryness in this case. Colour Dryness is White. Since we want to sedate it, we use colour Red (as Heat subjugates Dryness and the colour of Heat is Red). So we put Red dot on the CV Dryness point.

Super Six Ki : Yang organs

LI Dryness Sedation Fig 179

i. LI Dryness Sedation
ii. SI Heat Tonification
iii. LI Heat Tonification
iv. UB Coldness Sedation
v. LI Coldness Sedation
vi. SC Dryness Sedation
vii. GV Dryness Sedation

i. LI Dryness Sedation : Then see the colour of energy, that is Dryness in this case. Colour of Dryness is White. Since we want to sedate it, we use colour Red, as Heat subjugates Dryness. So we put red dot on the LI Dryness point.

ii. SI Heat Tonification : Then see the colour of next energy, that is Heat in this case. Colour of Heat is Red. Since we want to tonify it, we use colour Red. So we put Red dot on the SI Heat point.

iii. LI Heat Tonification : Then see the colour of energy, that is Heat in this case. Colour of Heat is Red. Since we want to tonification it, we use colour Red, as Heat subjugates Dryness. So we put red dot on the LI Heat point.

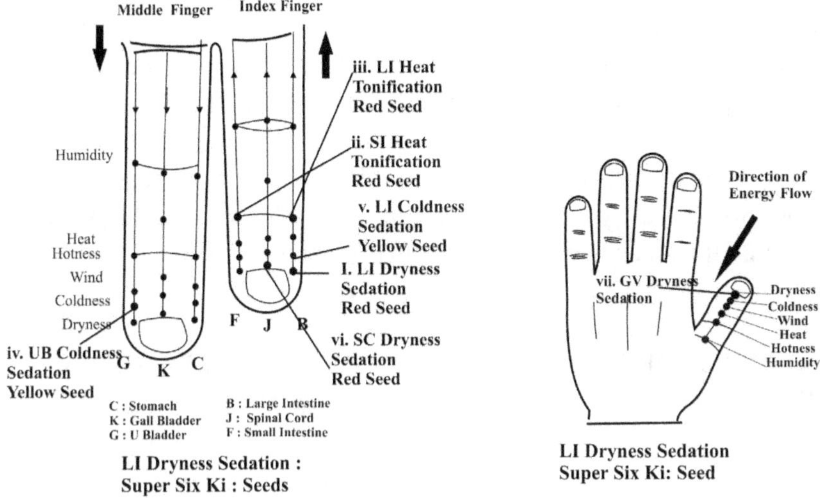

Fig. 179

iv. UB Coldness Sedation : Then see the colour of next energy, that is Coldness in this case. Colour of Coldness is Black. Since we want to sedate it, we use colour Yellow (as Humidity subjugates Coldness and the colour of Humidity is Yellow). So we put Black dot on the UB Coldness point.

v. LI Coldness Sedation: Then see the colour of next energy, that is Coldness. Colour of Coldness is Black. Since we want to sedate it, we use colour Yellow (as Humidity subjugates Coldness and the colour of Humidity is Yellow). So we put Yellow dot on the LI Coldness point.

vi. SC Dryness Sedation : Then see the colour of next energy, that is Dryness in this case. Colour Dryness is White. Since we want to sedate it, we use colour Red (as Heat subjugates Dryness and the colour of Heat is Red). So we put Red dot on the SC Dryness point.

vii. GV Dryness Sedation : Then see the colour of next energy, that is Dryness in this case. Colour Dryness is White. Since we want to sedate it, we use colour Red (as Heat subjugates Dryness and the colour of Heat is Red). So we put Red dot on the GV Dryness point.

I have given above use of seeds as per Six Ki - Original, Branch and Super Six Ki. Below I am giving formulae only for various diseases, although formulae have given in tabular form in the lesson.

EXAMPLES OF SEED APPLICATION FOR SOME DISEASES AS PER SIX KI

I am giving below some treatment formulae for various diseases. I am sure with the examples given above, with pictures, you can use seeds on the Six Ki, as per Original, Branch and Super Six Ki Methods. However, I am giving the colour also against each formula line. You have to put that colour seed on the Ki of the meridian.

Examples:

Liver Dryness sedation Red colour seed
So put Red colour seed on Liver Dryness Ki point.

Another example :
Lung Humidity Sedation Green colour seed
So put Green colour seed on Lung Humidity Ki point.

CATARACTS : are cloudy patches that develop in the lens of your eye and can cause blurred or misty vision.

Its symptoms are : blurred, cloudy or misty vision, or small spots or patches where your vision is less clear.

Branch Six Ki Method : Application of seeds
Liver Dryness sedation Red colour seed
Liver Heat tonification Red colour seed
Liver Coldness sedation Yellow colour seed
Brain Dryness sedation Red colour seed

EXCESSIVE COUGHING

Branch Six Ki Method : Application of seeds

Lung Humidity Sedation Greeen colour seed
Lung Wind Tonification Green colour seed

PLEURISY is a condition in which the layer covering the Lungs, called the Pleura, becomes inflamed. Common symptoms of pleurisy are sharp chest pain that feels worse with breathing, shortness of breath and a dry cough.

Pneumonia is inflammation (swelling) of the tissue in one or both of your Lungs. It is usually caused by an infection. The tiny air sacs get inflamed and filled up with fluid.

Its symptoms are : cough, fever, difficulty in breathing, muscle pains, headache, general weakness, pain in chest.

Original Six Ki Method :

SI Heat tonification Red colour seed
UB Coldness sedation Yellow colour seed
Stomach Humidity tonification Yellow colour seed
SC Heat tonification Red colour seed

Acute and General Digestive Disorders

Branch Six Ki Method :

Stomach Humidity Sedation
Stomach Wind Tonification
Stomach Dryness sedation
SC Humidity sedation

VOMITING :

Super Six Ki Method :

Stomach Humidity sedation
Stomach Wind tonification
GB Wind tonification
Stomach Dryness sedation
LI Dryness sedation
SC Humidity sedation
GV Humidity sedation

HYPER ACIDITY : It is a condition in which acidic contents of the stomach flow back into Oesopahgus and Mouth, accompanied by burning sensation behind the breast bone. The gastric juices secreted in the stomach aid in digestion and kill bacteria. But they contain acid which, when secreted in abnormal quantities, irritates the stomach lining and causes belching and a bitter taste in the mouth. Frequent acid indigestion can lead to gastric ulcers. Acidity is mainly caused due to uneven working of the liver.

Its symptoms are : Heartburn – burning chest pain or discomfort that occurs after eating, An unpleasant sour taste in the mouth – caused by stomach acid coming back up into the mouth (known as regurgitation), Dysphagia – pain and difficulty in swallowing.

Heartburn : Heartburn is a burning pain or a feeling of discomfort that develops just below your breastbone. The pain is usually worse after eating, or when bending over or lying down.

Original Six Ki Method :

Stomach Humidity sedation Green colour seed
GB Wind tonification Green colour seed
LI Dryness sedation Red colour seed
SC Humidity sedation Green colour seed

ALLERGY (skin rash)

Original Six Ki Method :

Lung Dryness sedation Red
Heart Heat tonification Red
Kidney Coldness sedation Yellow
Brain Dryness sedation Red

LEUCORRHEA : a yellowish or greenish white viscid discharge from the vagina resulting from inflammation or congestion of the uterine or vaginal mucous membrane.

Spleen Humidity sedation Green
CV Humidity sedation Green
    or

Spleen Coldness Tonification Black
CV Coldness tonification Black

MENOPAUSE, sometimes referred to as the "change of life", is the end of menstruation. That is, a woman's ovaries stop producing an egg every four weeks. Its symptoms are : hot flushes, night sweats, mood swings, vaginal dryness.

Its symptoms are : Feeling of hotness, no sweating, hot flushes

Heart Heat sedation Black
Brain Heat sedation Black

HEMORRHOIDS, also known as piles, are swellings that contain enlarged blood vessels that are found inside or around the bottom (the rectum and anus). Its symptoms are :bleeding after passing a stool (the blood will be bright red), itchy bottom, a lump hanging down outside of the anus, which may need to be pushed back in after passing a stool.

LI Humidity sedation Green
LI Wind tonification Green
LI Dryness sedation Red
SC Humidity sedation Green

BEDWETTING

UB Coldness sedation Yellow
UB Humidity tonification Yellow
UB Wind sedation White or Brown
SC Coldness sedation Yellow

SCIATICA PAIN : This is the name given to any sort of pain that is caused by irritation or compression of the sciatic nerve. The sciatic nerve is the longest nerve in your body. It runs from the back of your pelvis, through your buttocks, and all the way down both legs, ending at your feet. When something compresses or irritates the sciatic nerve, it can cause a pain that radiates out from your lower back and travels down your leg to your calf. Sciatic pain can range from being mild to very painful.

Spleen Humidity sedation Green
Liver Wind tonification Green
Lung Dryness sedation Red
Brain Humidity sedation Green

After this I am giving only the formulae. By this time you must have learnt the colours of the Six Ki, their tonification colour and sedation colour.

JOINTS AND MUSCLE PAINS

Liver Wind sedation
Joints and muscles are associated with Wind energy. Hence, original Liver Wind sedation.
With one clue, you can work out the complete formula for Liver Wind sedation.

Liver Wind sedation
Lung Dryness tonification
Heart Heat sedation
Brain Wind sedation

Headache (during study)

Brain sedation
SC tonification

Headache : UB Coldness sedation

Acute : Brain Wind Sedation
Brain Dryness Tonification

Chronic : Spleen Humidity Tonification
Kidney Coldness Sedation

Bladder Dryness Sedation
Bladder Heat Tonification

Acute Fever : Small Intestine Heat Sedation
Bladder Coldness Tonification

Chronic Fever : Heart Heat Sedation
Kidney Coldness Tonification

MIGRAINE : is usually a severe headache felt as a throbbing pain at the front or side of the head. Some people also have other symptoms, such as nausea, vomiting and increased sensitivity to light or sound.

GB sedation
Liver Wind sedation

Large Intestine Dryness Sedation
Large Intestine Heat Tonification

DE-ADDICTION OF TOBACCO/ SMOKING

Brain Heat (Desire) Sedation by Black
CV Heat sedation by Black

Brain Dryness (Will) Tonification by White
CV Dryness tonification by White

BRAIN TUMOUR : A benign (non-cancerous) brain tumour is a mass of cells that grows slowly in the brain. It usually stays in one place and does not spread.

The symptoms of a benign brain tumour depend on how big it is and where it is in the brain. Some slow-growing tumours may not cause any symptoms at first.

Eventually, the tumour can put pressure on the brain and may cause headaches and seizures (fits). The tumour can also prevent an area of the brain from functioning properly. For example, a tumour in the occipital lobe (at the back of the brain) may cause loss of vision on one side.

CV Dryness tonification by White

ACNE : Acne is a common skin condition that affects most people at some point. It causes spots to develop on the skin, usually on the face, back and chest. The spots can range from surface blackheads and whiteheads – which are often mild – to deep, inflamed, pus-filled pustules and cysts, which can be severe and long-lasting and lead to scarring.

Small Intestine sedation
Liver Heat sedation

EAR PROBLEMS

Earache is the result of an ear infection.
Earwax is a waxy material produced by sebaceous glands inside the ear. It cleans, lubricates and protects the lining of the ear by trapping dirt and repelling water. Earwax is slightly acidic and has antibacterial properties. Without earwax, the skin inside the ear would become dry, cracked, infected or waterlogged and sore. Earwax can be wet or dry, hard or soft.

Kidney Humidity sedation
Kidney Wind tonification
Kidney Dryness sedation
Brain Humidity sedation

Eye Problems

Gall Bladder Wind Tonification
Liver Hotness sedation

NIGHT BLINDNESS : reduced visual capacity in faint light (as at night).

Liver Coldness sedation

DRY EYES (NO TEAR)

Liver Heat sedation
Liver Coldness tonification

STYE : is a small abscess (painful collection of pus) on the eyelid. It appears as a painful lump on the outside or inside of the eyelid.

Its symptoms are : A watery eye, A red eye or eyelid.
Spleen Coldness Tonification

When it Is Difficult to Move Eyebrows
Since eyes are associated with Wind,

Liver Wind sedation

Ptosis (drooping of the upper eyelid due to damage of the oculomotor nerve)
GB Wind tonification

When the Sclera of Eyes Appears Yellow
Liver Humidity sedation

When Eyes Twitch Repeatedly
Gall Bladder Wind Sedation

Itchy and Aching Eyes
Liver Dryness or Wind Sedation

Swollen Eyes
Liver Hotness Sedation
Liver Humidity Sedation

More Tears
Liver Humidity Sedation (Liver is also associated with tears)

Painful Eyes
Liver Dryness Sedation
Liver Heat Tonification

Red and Swollen Eyes
Spleen Hotness Sedation

RED EYES
Liver Heat Sedation
Liver Coldness tonification

LONG-SIGHTEDNESS : If you are long-sighted, you find it hard to see things close-up.

GB Dryness sedation

SHORT-SIGHTEDNESS : If you are short-sighted, distance vision is blurred.
Liver Hotness sedation
Liver Coldness tonification

MOUTH ULCERS
Mouth ulcers are painful round or oval sores that form in the

mouth, most often on the inside of the cheeks or lips. They're usually white, red, yellow or grey in colour and are inflamed (red and swollen) around the edge.

Stomach Heat sedation
Stomach Coldness tonification
Stomach Humidity sedation
SC Heat sedation

Since ulceration is associated with Dryness,
LI Dryness sedation

TONSILLITIS is inflammation of the tonsils. It's usually caused by a viral infection or, less commonly, a bacterial infection.

The tonsils play a role in protecting the body against respiratory and gastrointestinal infections. Its symptoms are : Sore throat that can feel worse when swallowing, High temperature, Coughing, Headache.

Spleen Heat or Hotness Sedation
Spleen Coldness Tonification

Heart Dryness Sedation
Heart Heat Tonification

Lung Dryness Sedation

Stomach Hotness Sedation
Stomach Coldness tonification

GUM SWELLING (PUS)

Stomach Humidity sedation

LARYNGITIS is inflammation of the larynx (voice box). In most cases, it will get better without treatment in about a week.

Its symptoms are : Hoarse voice, Difficulty in speaking, Sore throat, Mild fever, Irritating cough, A constant need to clear your throat. Lung Dryness sedation (as Lung is associated with throat)

HYPERTHYROIDISM (Overactive thyroid) is a relatively common hormonal condition that occurs when there is too much thyroid hormone in the body. Excess levels of thyroid hormones can then speed up the body's metabolism triggering a range of symptoms, such as:

Nervousness and anxiety
Hyperactivity – where a person can't stay still and is full of nervous energy
Unexplained or unplanned weight loss
Swelling of the thyroid gland, which causes a noticeable lump known as a goitre to form in the throat

Heart Heat sedation by Black
Heart Coldness tonification by Black
Heart Humidity sedation by Green
Brain Heat sedation by Black

HYPOTHYROIDISM (An underactive thyroid) means thyroid gland does not produce enough hormones.

Common signs of an underactive thyroid are tiredness, weight gain and feeling depressed.

Heart Heat tonification by Red
Heart Coldness sedation by Yellow
Heart Humidity tonification by Yellow
Brain Heat tonification by Red

Clogged nose :
Lung Hotness Sedation
Lung Coldness Tonification

Mucus :
Lung Dryness Tonification
Spleen Humidity Sedation

ALLERGIC RHINITIS is inflammation of the inside of the nose caused by an allergen, such as pollen, dust, mould or flakes of skin from certain animals.

LI Humidity sedation

Wet Cough :Lung Humidity Sedation
Lung Wind Tonification

Dry Cough : Lung Dryness sedation
Lung Heat tonification

COUGHING WITH EXCESSIVE PHLEGM

Lung Coldness Tonification
Lung Humidity Sedation

PLEURISY is a condition in which the layer covering the Lungs, called the Pleura, becomes inflamed. Common symptoms of pleurisy are sharp chest pain that feels worse with breathing, shortness of breath and a dry cough.

Pneumonia is inflammation (swelling) of the tissue in one or both of your Lungs. It is usually caused by an infection. The tiny air sacs get inflamed and filled up with fluid.

Its symptoms are : cough, fever, difficulty in breathing, muscle pains, headache, general weakness, pain in chest.

SI Heat tonification by Red
UB Coldness sedation by Yellow
Stomach Humidity tonification by Green
SC Heat tonification by Red

TUBERCULOSIS (TB) is a bacterial infection spread through inhaling tiny droplets from the coughs or sneezes of an infected person. It is a serious condition but can be cured with proper treatment. TB mainly affects the lungs. However, it can affect any part of the body, including the bones and nervous system.

Its symptoms are : Having a persistent cough for more than three weeks that brings up phlegm, which may be bloody, Weight loss, Night sweats, High temperature (fever), Tiredness and fatigue, Loss of appetite.

Lung Dryness Tonification
Lung Heat Sedation

ASTHMA is a common long-term condition that can cause a cough, wheezing, and breathlessness. Asthma is caused by inflammation of the airways. These are the small tubes, called bronchi, which carry air in and out of the lungs.

Dyspnoea : Sensation of lack of air accompanied by disturbance of respiration frequency and depth. Acute dyspnoea is called asphyxia.

If you have problem in breathing, first find out whether the problem is in inhaling or exhaling.

Lung Dryness Sedation
Lung Heat Tonification

Breathing Problem : Inhaling

Kidney Dryness sedation
Kidney Heat Tonification

BRONCHIAL ASTHMA : Asthma resulting from spasmodic contraction of bronchial muscles.

Lungs Humidity sedation
Lungs Wind Tonification
Lungs Dryness sedation
Brain Humidity sedation

CARDIAC ASTHMA : Asthma due to heart disease (as heart failure) that occurs in paroxysms usually at night and is characterized by difficult wheezing respiration, pallor, and anxiety.

Iahs Courses

Diploma in Sujok Therapy
Advance Diploma in Sujok Therapy
Master Diploma in Sujok Therapy
Diploma in Sujok Therapy (Hindi)
Diploma in Seeds Therapy

Video and Text lessons are sent through email.
For any query/doubts you can write to me.

Diploma in .pdf format is sent through email.

You can see the details of all courses, e.g. syllabus, fee, etc, on our site www.doctorasethi.com

Or write to me at doctorasethi@gmail.com
or call me on 01149326765 or 9625723446
or WhatsApp to 9811047247.

Iahs Courses

Reiki Mastership (Level I, II and III a/b)
Reiki Grandmastership (Level IVA)
Reiki Grandmastership Karmic (Level IVB)
Reiki Grandmastership (Levels V to XX)
Violet Flame Reiki Mastership
Angelic Reiki Mastership
Money Reiki Grandmastership
Lama Fera Grandmastership
Diploma in Bach Flowers Therpy

Video and Text lessons are sent through email.
For any query/doubts you can write to me.

Diploma in .pdf format is sent through email.

You can see the details of all courses, e.g. syllabus,
fee, etc, on our site www.doctorasethi.com

Or write to me at doctorasethi@gmail.com
or call me on 01149326765 or 9625723446
or WhatsApp to 9811047247.

Iahs Courses

Diploma in Astrology
Advance Diploma in Astrology
Master Diploma in Astrology
Diploma in Palmistry
Diploma in Numerology
Diploma in Tarot Reading

Text lessons are sent through email.
For any query/doubts you can write to me.

Diploma in .pdf format is sent through email.

You can see the details of all courses, e.g. syllabus, fee, etc, on our site www.doctorasethi.com

Or write to me at doctorasethi@gmail.com or call me on 01149326765 or 9625723446 or WhatsApp to 9811047247.

Iahs Courses

Diploma in Ayurvedic Acupressure
Ho'onoponopono Healer
Jin Shin Jyutsu Healer
Emotional Frequency Tapping
Diploma in Mudra Therapy
Diploma in Bach Flowers Therapy

*Video and Text lessons are sent through email.
For any query/doubts you can write to me.*

Diploma in .pdf format is sent through email.

*You can see the details of all courses, e.g. syllabus,
fee, etc, on our site www.doctorasethi.com*

*Or write to me at doctorasethi@gmail.com
or call me on 01149326765 or 9625723446
or WhatsApp to 9811047247.*

Our Books

1. Sujok Correspondence Points
2. Sujok Therapy
3. Advance Sujok Therapy (Part 1 of 2)
4. Advance Sujok Therapy (Part 2 of 2)
5. Master Sujok Therapy (Part 1 of 2)
6. Master Sujok Therapy (Part 2 of 2)
7. Lama Fera Grandmastrship
8. Reiki Mastership
9. Money Reiki Grandmastershi
10. Astrology Made Simple (Part 1 of 3)
11. Astrology Made Simple (Part 2 of 3)
12. Astrology Made Simple (Part 3 of 3)
13. Diploma in Art of Dowsing
14. Mudra Therapy
15. Violet Flame and Angel Reiki Mastership
16. Bach Flowers Remedies (also at **amazon.com, amazon.co.uk** and e-kindle (international)

Available on Amazon, Flipkart and Notion Press Store

9 798890 664082